CONSTITUTIONAL
AMENDMENTS
BEYOND THE BILL OF RIGHTS

Amendment XIII
Abolishing Slavery

Other Books of Related Interest

Opposing Viewpoints Series

Civil Liberties

Feminism

Race Relations

Work

Working Women

Current Controversies Series

Civil Liberties

Extremist Groups

Feminism

Human Rights

★ CONSTITUTIONAL
AMENDMENTS
BEYOND THE BILL OF RIGHTS

Amendment XIII
Abolishing Slavery

Tracey Biscontini and Rebecca Sparling, Book Editors

GREENHAVEN PRESS
A part of Gale, Cengage Learning

Detroit • New York • San Francisco • New Haven, Conn • Waterville, Maine • London

GALE
CENGAGE Learning™

Christine Nasso, *Publisher*
Elizabeth Des Chenes, *Managing Editor*

© 2009 Greenhaven Press, a part of Gale, Cengage Learning.

Gale and Greenhaven Press are registered trademarks used herein under license.

For more information, contact:
Greenhaven Press
27500 Drake Rd.
Farmington Hills, MI 48331-3535
Or you can visit our Internet site at gale.cengage.com

For product information and technology assistance, contact us at

Gale Customer Support, 1-800-877-4253
For permission to use material from this text or product, submit all requests online at www.cengage.com/permissions

Further permissions questions can be emailed to permissionrequest@cengage.com

Articles in Greenhaven Press anthologies are often edited for length to meet page requirements. In addition, original titles of these works are changed to clearly present the main thesis and to explicitly indicate the author's opinion. Every effort is made to ensure that Greenhaven Press accurately reflects the original intent of the authors. Every effort has been made to trace the owners of copyrighted material.

Cover photograph copyright Hulton Archive/Getty Images.

LIBRARY OF CONGRESS CATALOGING-IN-PUBLICATION DATA

Amendment XIII : abolishing slavery / Tracey Biscontini and Rebecca Sparling, book editors.
  p. cm. -- (Constitutional amendments: beyond the Bill of Rights)
  Includes bibliographical references and index.
  ISBN 978-0-7377-4122-3 (hardcover)
  1. Slavery--Law and legislation--United States. 2. Constitutional amendments--United States--13th. 3. United States. Constitution. 13th Amendment--History. 4. Constitutional amendments--United States. I. Biscontini, Tracey Vasil. II. Sparling, Rebecca. III. Title: Amendment thirteen. IV. Title: Amendment 13.
  KF4545.S5A9494 2009
  342.7308'7--dc22

                                                      2008032032

Printed in the United States of America
2 3 4 5 6 7 12 11 10

Contents

Chapter 1: Historical Background on the Thirteenth Amendment

Chapter 3: Current Debate on Slavery and Its Impact on Modern Life

Appendices

Amendment XIII: Abolishing Slavery

> *"Today's Constitution is a realistic docu-*
> *ment of freedom only because of several*
> *corrective amendments. Those amend-*
> *ments speak to a sense of decency and*
> *fairness."*
>
> *Thurgood Marshall*

While the U.S. Constitution forms the backbone of American democracy, the amendments make the Constitution a living, ever-evolving document. Interpretation and analysis of the Constitution inform lively debate in every branch of government, as well as among students, scholars, and all other citizens, and views on various articles of the Constitution have changed over the generations. Formally altering the Constitution, however, can happen only through the amendment process. The Greenhaven Press series The Bill of Rights examines the first ten amendments to the Constitution. Constitutional Amendments: Beyond the Bill of Rights continues the exploration, addressing key amendments ratified since 1791.

The process of amending the Constitution is painstaking. While other options are available, the method used for nearly every amendment begins with a congressional bill that must pass both the Senate and the House of Representatives by a two-thirds majority. Then the amendment must be ratified by three-quarters of the states. Many amendments have been proposed since the Bill of Rights was adopted in 1791, but only seventeen have been ratified.

It may be difficult to imagine a United States where women and African Americans are prohibited from voting, where the federal government allows one human being to enslave another, or where some citizens are denied equal protection under the law. While many of our most fundamental liberties are protected by the Bill of Rights, the amendments that followed have significantly broadened and enhanced the rights of American citizens. Such rights may be taken for granted today, but when the amendments were ratified, many were considered groundbreaking and proved to be explosively controversial.

Each volume in Constitutional Amendments provides an in-depth exploration of an amendment and its impact through primary and secondary sources, both historical and contemporary. Primary sources include landmark Supreme Court rulings, speeches by prominent experts, and newspaper editorials. Secondary sources include historical analyses, law journal articles, book excerpts, and magazine articles. Each volume first presents the historical background of the amendment, creating a colorful picture of the circumstances surrounding the amendment's passage: the campaigns to sway public opinion, the congressional debates, and the struggle for ratification. Next, each volume examines the ways the court system has been used to test the validity of the amendment and addresses the ramifications of the amendment's passage. The final chapter of each volume presents viewpoints that explore current controversies and debates relating to ways in which the amendment affects our everyday lives.

Numerous features are included in each Constitutional Amendments volume:

- An originally written introduction presents a concise yet thorough overview of the amendment.

- A time line provides historical context by describing key events, organizations, and people relating to the ratification of the amendment, subsequent court cases, and the impact of the amendment.

- An annotated table of contents offers an at-a-glance summary of each primary and secondary source essay included in the volume.

- The complete text of the amendment, followed by a "plain English" explanation, brings the amendment into clear focus for students and other readers.

- Graphs, charts, tables, and maps enhance the text.

- A list of all twenty-seven Constitutional Amendments offers quick reference.

- An annotated list of court cases relevant to the amendment broadens the reader's understanding of the judiciary's role in interpreting the Constitution.

- A bibliography of books, periodicals, and Web sites aids readers in further research.

- A detailed subject index allows readers to quickly find the information they need.

With the aid of this series, students and other researchers will become better informed of their rights and responsibilities as American citizens. Constitutional Amendments: Beyond the Bill of Rights examines the roots of American democracy, bringing to life the ways the Constitution has evolved and how it has impacted this nation's history.

Amendment Text and Explanation

The Thirteenth Amendment to the United States Constitution

Passed by Congress January 31, 1865. Ratified December 6, 1865.

Note: A portion of Article IV, section 2, of the Constitution was superseded by the Thirteenth Amendment.

Section 1. Neither slavery nor involuntary servitude, except as a punishment for crime whereof the party shall have been duly convicted, shall exist within the United States, or any place subject to their jurisdiction.

Section 2. Congress shall have the power to enforce this article by appropriate legislation.

Explanation

This transcript of the Thirteenth Amendment clearly indicates that the government intended the amendment to abolish slavery, in all its forms, within the United States and its territories. The only exception would be in the incident of incarceration or community service. The amendment also gives Congress the power to uphold this law through legislative action.

Though the Thirteenth Amendment seems self-explanatory, the language used in the amendment is both vague and broad. Though Section 1 gives freedom to all slaves within the United States and its territories, it does not guarantee these former slaves equal treatment under the law. As a result, the former Confederate states enacted the so-called Black Codes. The codes were a form of social control that limited the rights of freed slaves in the Southern states. Depending on a state's law, former slaves were denied the right to own property and were often discriminated against by employers. Southern states argued that though the Thirteenth Amendment gave slaves their freedom, it did not give them citizenship. This debate would eventually lead to the creation of the Fourteenth Amendment, which provided blacks with citizenship and guaranteed that they would be treated equally under federal and state laws.

The language used in Section 2 was also of issue. Several Supreme Court cases, including *Hodges v. United States*, would test the scope of Congress's power to enforce Section 1 of the amendment. Questions of whether Congress had the authority to regulate acts of discrimination among communities and private businesses under the amendment would be a point of contention in several instances.

Nevertheless, the straightforward language of the Thirteenth Amendment does fulfill its intended purpose: abolishing slavery within the United States.

Introduction

Though most people know that the Thirteenth Amendment abolished slavery and indentured servitude in the United States, few understand the effort it took to amend the Constitution. Arguments about slavery began when the first Africans arrived on American soil. From that moment on, the issue divided families and communities and nearly destroyed the Union.

The fight for the Thirteenth Amendment is arguably one of the most dramatic and deadly of the Constitution. The battle against slavery not only encompassed issues of civil rights but also raised questions over the power of the federal government versus the power of individual states and started one of the bloodiest wars in American history. The text of the amendment itself is brief, but the history of the Thirteenth Amendment is long and complex.

Slavery Becomes Part of the New World

Even before the Pilgrims landed at Plymouth Rock, slavery found its way to the shores of the New World. The colonists of Jamestown, Virginia, raised several types of crops, including tobacco. Tobacco's popularity in England allowed Jamestown to flourish. Tobacco quickly became the most valuable crop in the colony. Raising tobacco was a difficult task, and overseas demand for the crop increased the need for permanent, inexpensive labor. In 1619 Jamestown colonists purchased twenty African slaves from a passing Dutch ship. This exchange marked the inauspicious start of slavery in the New World. The North American slave trade was launched shortly thereafter when the first American slave carrier set sail for Africa in 1636.

While many Europeans fled to America to escape religious persecution, most seemed willing to inflict slavery upon captive Africans. To justify this hypocrisy, many of these groups argued that slaves were in some way inferior to Europeans and were therefore destined for servitude. Some argued that slavery had existed since the beginning of time and would most likely continue throughout human history.

Others recognized the ills of slavery almost immediately. Several religious groups opposed slavery in all its forms. The Quakers adopted the first resolution against slavery in 1688. They held that slavery was in direct opposition to Christianity and to basic human rights.

Such groups as the Quakers, however, were in the minority in their beliefs about slavery. As the population grew and as demands for cheap labor increased, the colonies quickly legalized slavery. Small pockets of abolitionists continued to fight for the freedom of slaves, though, even when it seemed like a lost cause.

As slavery became more widespread, the slaves themselves suffered more atrocities. Several colonies adopted fugitive slave laws that allowed slave owners to cross state lines to retrieve runaway slaves. Recaptured slaves often suffered severe punishment for disobeying their masters. Some slave owners even forced slaves to give up their personal religious beliefs and convert to Christianity.

While slavery continued to flourish in the colonies, attitudes were changing in Great Britain. Such British abolitionists as Thomas Clarkson and Granville Sharpe helped expose the barbarity of the transatlantic slave trade. Their work eventually led to the abolition of the slave trade through the 1807 Slave Trade Act, which prevented Great Britain from participating in the transatlantic slave trade. Though it took another thirty years to abolish slavery completely in the country, American abolitionists saw the legislation as a victory for antislavery groups around the world.

A Series of Compromises

Over the course of the next century, the debate over slavery continued to intensify. During the eighteenth century abolitionism gained ground as several states outlawed the importation of slaves. Vermont became the first state to outlaw slavery entirely after the Revolutionary War. Other Northern states followed soon after with gradual emancipation laws. However, just as Northern states started to shy away from slavery, Southern states began to dig in their heels.

Many people in the South were farmers who depended on cheap labor to keep their plantations running. Southerners viewed abolition as a direct threat to their livelihood, causing a deep rift between the North and the South.

Sensing that the tension between the regions would only worsen, government officials designed a series of compromises to try to hold the Union together for as long as possible. The first major compromise was the Northwest Ordinance of 1787. At first glance it does not seem like much of a compromise. The ordinance banned slavery in the Northwest Territory (Ohio, Indiana, Illinois, Michigan, and Wisconsin) except as punishment for a crime. Any slaves who escaped to the territory, however, would be returned to their masters.

The next major compromise was the U.S. Constitution. Because the framers of the Constitution wanted to get the Constitution ratified and to avoid conflict among the states, the original text did not address the issue of slavery. The Constitution also allowed that three-fifths of the number of slaves in a state would count toward that state's population for purposes of taxation and representation in the Congress.

In 1803 the United States purchased the Louisiana Territory from the French government. Northerners and Southerners wondered how the newly acquired region would deal with the issue of slavery. Again the government tried to come up with a plan to satisfy both sides. Under the Missouri Compromise of 1820, Missouri entered the Union as a slave state and

Maine as a free state, to keep a balance. Under these terms slavery was outlawed in the Louisiana Territory north of Missouri's southern border, except for in the state of Missouri.

As the Union expanded its borders westward, the fight to keep the balance between free and slave states continued. Pieces of legislation, such as the Compromise of 1850, attempted to keep peace between the states.

Maintaining peace became more difficult as the fight for freedom intensified. Slave rebellions caused outrage among white slave owners in the South. At the same time, efforts to bring abolition to the forefront increased only throughout the North. In the 1830s a wave of abolitionist leaders, such as William Lloyd Garrison and Wendell Phillips, tackled the issue of slavery head-on. Newspapers and magazines devoted to the abolitionist movement sprang up across the country. Supporters held conventions in the hopes of prompting lawmakers to push for a federal law against slavery. There were setbacks, of course. In 1857 the Supreme Court ruling in the *Dred Scott* case denied citizenship to all slaves, former slaves, and descendants of slaves. The Court also ruled that Congress could not outlaw slavery in the territories.

Proslavery groups also received a blow. In 1860 Abraham Lincoln was elected president of the United States. This spark set off the Southern powder keg.

The Election of Lincoln: The Beginning of the End

Though Lincoln never called for the abolition of slavery during his presidential campaign, it was general knowledge that he opposed the institution. Lincoln's views were distasteful to Southerners. Throughout the election, rumors of secession spread throughout the South. When it became clear that Lincoln would win the presidency, Southern states started calling for conventions to discuss the issue of seceding from the Union.

South Carolina was the first to secede. On December 24, 1860, the people declared their right to secede from the Union based on "the frequent violations of the Constitution of the United States, by the Federal Government, and its encroachments upon the reserved rights of the States." Several other states soon followed in South Carolina's footsteps.

As the states seceded, the issue of slavery took a backseat to the preservation of the Union. Lincoln believed that secession was illegal. The new president was willing to do whatever was necessary to uphold federal law and to preserve the Union. The Confederate States of America formed during the first months of Lincoln's term in office.

War loomed on the horizon. The Civil War erupted when Confederate soldiers seized federal forts throughout the South. As the war raged on, Lincoln issued the Emancipation Proclamation, freeing all slaves in Confederate territories. Many criticized the president's actions—even his own secretary of state, William Seward, who commented, "We show our sympathy with slavery by emancipating slaves where we cannot reach them and holding them in bondage where we can set them free." Lincoln recognized the flaws of the proclamation but did not wish to anger slave states still loyal to the Union.

During the next few years, Lincoln outlined a plan for reconstruction that would allow Confederate states to rejoin the Union after swearing loyalty oaths and accepting the abolition of slavery. Even as the war continued, Lincoln hoped that he would see the country united under one flag again.

At the same time, members of Congress proposed a constitutional amendment banning slavery. In February 1864 the Senate approved an amendment abolishing slavery in the United States. The amendment had a long and difficult journey ahead. The House still needed to approve the amendment by a two-thirds majority. It took almost a year and three votes for the House to approve the Thirteenth Amendment. In February 1865 states started the ratification process.

Shortly after the states began the process of abolishing slavery, the Civil War ended. Although some people hoped that the Confederate states would rejoin the Union, the country was still deeply divided, and the damage seemed unlikely to be easily repaired. Just as the country was getting back on its feet, the American people were dealt another tragedy. The Confederate supporter John Wilkes Booth assassinated Lincoln. The country was left without a leader in a time of great conflict.

Reconstruction and the Impact of the Thirteenth Amendment

After Lincoln's death, Americans struggled to repair the fractured Union. Andrew Johnson took over the presidency, and states continued to ratify the Thirteenth Amendment. The passage of the amendment did not erase the country's color lines, however. While the Thirteenth Amendment abolished slavery, it did not grant former slaves full citizenship. Southerners, angry over the war's outcome, established a series of laws called the Black Codes. These laws, created at the state and local level, restricted the civil liberties of black Americans living in the South. Even though the Fourteenth Amendment, passed in 1868, afforded the right of full citizenship to all former slaves, the battle for equality was only beginning.

Many white communities continued to restrict freedoms by establishing separate public facilities for blacks. Races were segregated in schools, on buses, and even in public restrooms. Homer Plessy made the first attempt to fight segregation using the Constitution. In the case of *Plessy v. Ferguson*, the Supreme Court ruled that "separate but equal" facilities did not violate the Thirteenth or Fourteenth Amendment. This decision increased racial tensions for years to come.

It took the Supreme Court more than sixty years to overturn the decision made in *Plessy v. Ferguson*. In 1954 the Court heard the case of *Brown v. Board of Education of Topeka, Kansas*. The main argument in *Brown* stated that public facilities for blacks were not equal to those provided to whites and that segregation only perpetuated racial discrimination throughout the United States. In a unanimous decision, the Court found that state laws establishing "separate but equal" facilities for blacks violated the Fourteenth Amendment.

This decision was a huge victory, but the fight for civil rights continued. For more than a decade, reform movements swept across the United States. Groups called on government officials to enact legislation that would end discrimination. Their tireless efforts paid off when President Lyndon Johnson signed the Civil Rights Act of 1964, prohibiting segregation and discrimination in public facilities, in the government, and in hiring practices.

Though many people view the Thirteenth Amendment as a historical document, it is still alive in many ways. It has been instrumental in the decisions of several Supreme Court cases over the years, including *Jones v. Mayer Co.* (1968) and *Memphis v. Greene* (1981). The amendment was also significant in the Victims of Trafficking and Violence Act of 2000, which worked to combat trafficking of persons into the sex trade, slavery, and indentured servitude.

The Thirteenth Amendment was the foundation of several other amendments, including the Fourteenth and Fifteenth Amendments. One could also argue that it opened the door for the women's suffrage movement. The impact of the Thirteenth Amendment continues to be felt throughout the world, inspiring other nations to enact similar laws banning human slavery. This amendment continues to protect the fundamental rights of people.

Chronology

1612
The first tobacco crop is raised in Jamestown, Virginia.

1619
Twenty captive Africans arrive in the colonies and are sold as slaves to work on plantations.

1641
Massachusetts is the first colony to legalize slavery.

1652
Rhode Island is the first colony to place restrictions on slavery. These restrictions prohibit a person from being enslaved for more than ten years.

1654
A Virginia court grants blacks the right to hold slaves.

1657
Virginia passes a fugitive slave law that allows citizens to cross state lines to bring back runaway slaves.

1662
Virginia passes the Hereditary Slavery Law, which states that any child born to an enslaved woman will inherit the mother's slave status.

1688
In Germantown, Pennsylvania, Quakers and Mennonites protest slavery. These groups pass the first formal antislavery resolution among their members.

1694
Rice cultivation is introduced to the colonies, increasing the demand for slaves.

1696

New England colonists enter the slave trade after the Royal African Trade Company loses its monopoly.

1705

The Virginia Slave Code defines all slaves as real estate.

1712

Pennsylvania prohibits the importation of slaves.

An alleged slave riot in New York leads to the death of nine white men and the execution of eighteen slaves.

1733

The Quaker Elihu Coleman publishes *A Testimony Against the Anti-Christian Practice of Making Slaves of Men.*

1774

The First Continental Congress bans trade with Britain and vows to discontinue the slave trade.

Connecticut, Rhode Island, and Georgia pass their own laws prohibiting the importation of slaves by state citizens.

1775

The first abolition society is established in Philadelphia, Pennsylvania.

The Revolutionary War begins.

Black minutemen join the fight against the British.

1776

The Declaration of Independence is signed.

1777–1780

Vermont, New York, Rhode Island, Virginia, Delaware, Pennsylvania, and Massachusetts take steps toward abolishing or restricting slavery in their states.

1787

The Northwest Ordinance forbids slavery, except as criminal punishment, in the Northwest Territory. Several states also prohibit their citizens from participating in the slave trade.

The U.S. Constitution is drafted in Philadelphia, Pennsylvania. The issue of slavery is not directly addressed. To keep the peace among the states, a compromise is reached, allowing three-fifths of the number of slaves in a state to count toward the state's population for taxation and representation purposes.

1793

Eli Whitney's invention of the cotton gin makes cotton production more profitable and increases the value of and demand for slaves.

1794

Congress prohibits slave trade with foreign countries.

1803

The United States purchases the Louisiana Territory from France.

1820

The Missouri Compromise allows Missouri to enter the Union as a slave state and Maine to enter as a free state. The compromise also prohibits slavery in the rest of the Louisiana Purchase north of 36° 30' latitude.

1834–1835

Anti-abolition riots break out in cities up and down the East Coast.

1842

In the case of *Prigg v. Pennsylvania*, the U.S. Supreme Court rules that the 1793 Fugitive Slave Law is constitutional. It also holds that personal liberty laws make unconstitutional demands on slave owners. The Court rules that enforcement of the Fugitive Slave Law is the responsibility of the federal government and is not up to the individual states.

1843

Several states pass their own personal liberty laws in response to the Supreme Court ruling in *Prigg v. Pennsylvania.*

1850

The Compromise of 1850 admits California to the Union as a free state. The territories of Utah and New Mexico are open to slavery on the basis of popular sovereignty (the vote of residents). The slave trade, but not slavery itself, is abolished in the District of Columbia. The compromise holds that the slave state of Texas would also have to give up its claim to land within the New Mexico Territory.

1854

The Kansas-Nebraska Act establishes the territories of Kansas and Nebraska. In an effort to encourage western expansion, the issue of slavery is to be decided by popular sovereignty. This act repeals the law established by the Missouri Compromise stating that slavery would be prohibited in the Louisiana Purchase north of 36° 30' latitude.

1857

The *Dred Scott* case is heard before the U.S. Supreme Court. Dred Scott is a slave who traveled through free states with his master. After his master's death, Scott sues for his freedom, arguing that the time he spent in free territories makes him free. The Court denies citizenship to Scott, all former slaves, and the descendents of slaves. It also denies Congress the right to prohibit slavery in the territories.

1860

Abraham Lincoln is elected president. Fearing that the election of Lincoln will accelerate the emancipation of slaves, South Carolina votes to secede from the Union on December 20.

1861

Mississippi, Florida, Alabama, Georgia, Louisiana, Texas, Virginia, North Carolina, Arkansas, and Tennessee also secede. These states later form the Union of Confederate States, led by President Jefferson Davis. The Civil War begins when Confederate troops take over the federal fort off the coast of Charleston, South Carolina.

1862

Lincoln and other lawmakers offer the Confederate states gradual, compensated emancipation of slaves in an effort to repair the Union. This proposal is rejected. In turn, Congress bans slavery in Washington, D.C., and the territories.

1863

President Lincoln signs the Emancipation Proclamation. This document declares all slaves in Confederate-held territory free.

Lincoln proposes a reconstruction plan that offers amnesty to white Southerners who take loyalty oaths to the Union and accept the abolishment of slavery.

Congressman James Ashley proposes a bill in support of an abolition amendment. Other members of Congress rally around the idea of a constitutional amendment to abolish slavery.

1864

Congress puts forth a proposal for reconstruction, stipulating that only those who swear that they never fought against the Union will be allowed to participate in the reconstruction of state governments. President Lincoln refuses to sign the bill, fearing that it will derail his own plans for reconstruction. Later this year the governments of Louisiana, Arkansas, and Tennessee are reconstructed under Lincoln's original plan.

Senator John Henderson submits a joint resolution calling for an amendment to abolish slavery. Other members of Congress present similar proposals.

1865

The Civil War ends in April when Confederates surrender to Union soldiers.

President Lincoln is assassinated by the Confederate sympathizer John Wilkes Booth days after the war's end. Vice President Andrew Johnson is sworn in as the seventeenth president.

Congress passes the Thirteenth Amendment to the U.S. Constitution, abolishing slavery and indentured servitude throughout the United States. Individual states start the process of ratifying the amendment.

1866

President Johnson vetoes a supplemental bill to expand the Freedmen's Bureau, as well as a bill that would extend civil rights to black males. The veto increases the stress between Congress and the president.

The Fourteenth Amendment is sent to the states. This amendment gives citizenship to all persons born or naturalized in the United States. It also expands the federal government's power over the states to protect the rights of citizens. The amendment will take more than two years to be ratified.

1867

The period known as "Radical Reconstruction" begins. Congress passes harsher reconstruction laws, turning some former states into military districts. It also contends that these areas must ratify the Fourteenth Amendment.

1868

Congress impeaches President Johnson. He narrowly avoids removal.

Several states are readmitted to the Union.

1869

Ulysses S. Grant is elected president.

1870

The Fifteenth Amendment holds that no U.S. government can deny a citizen the right to vote based on race, color, or previous condition of servitude.

1873

The Supreme Court hears a block of cases known as the *Slaughter-House Cases*. These cases are viewed as pivotal to early civil rights. The Court decides that the Thirteenth and Fourteenth Amendments do not guarantee federal protection of individual rights against discrimination by their own state governments.

1896

In the case of *Plessy v. Ferguson*, the Supreme Court rules that "separate but equal" treatment is constitutional.

1908

Bailey v. Alabama goes before the Supreme Court. Alonzo Bailey is an African American who agreed to work for twelve dollars a month and was paid a fifteen-dollar advance. He stopped working after one month but did not refund any of the money. An Alabama court finds Bailey guilty of trying to defraud his employer. The case is appealed all the way to the Supreme Court. The justices hold that finding a person guilty of taking money for work not performed is equivalent to indentured servitude, which is illegal under the Thirteenth Amendment because it requires Bailey to work rather than to be found guilty of a crime.

1916

Another case goes before the Supreme Court, narrowing the scope of the Thirteenth Amendment. *Butler v. Perry* challenges a Florida law that holds that every able-bodied man over the age of twenty-one is required to work on repairing public roads or to pay a small tax. The Court holds that because the men had the option of paying the tax, the law cannot be considered indentured servitude and is legal.

1954

The case of *Brown v. Board of Education* overturns the Court's ruling in *Plessy v. Ferguson*. The Court holds that separate-but-equal schools for African American children are inherently unequal and put the children at a disadvantage.

1955–1968

Reform movements throughout the United States aim to end racial discrimination against African Americans.

President Lyndon Johnson signs the Civil Rights Act of 1964 into law, outlawing segregation in public schools and places.

1969

In the case of *Jones v. Mayer*, the Supreme Court finds that Congress has the right to regulate the sale of private property to prevent discrimination.

1981

The City of Memphis, Tennessee, closes a road that connects a predominately white neighborhood to a predominately black neighborhood. In the case of *Memphis v. Greene*, the Supreme Court holds that the city's decision is not intended to disenfranchise African Americans and does not give white citizens any advantage.

2000

The Victims of Trafficking and Violence Protection Act of 2000 is established to combat trafficking of persons into the sex trade, slavery, and indentured servitude. The act gives Congress the power to establish programs to assist victims.

CHAPTER 1

Historical Background on the Thirteenth Amendment

A Historical Defense of Slavery

Thomas R. Dew

In 1831 Nat Turner, a slave, led a bloody rebellion against white slave owners in Virginia. As the rebels fought to release the slaves, they murdered about sixty slave owners. The quickly quashed rebellion led to a fierce debate over the issue of slavery in the Virginia legislature. Many members of this governing body questioned whether abolishing slavery would prevent future violence. In his response to this debate, Professor Thomas R. Dew of William and Mary College argues that slavery is a practice almost as old as time itself. Dew feels that slavery is not only a right but also an important factor in preventing prisoners of war from being murdered by their captors. The professor uses historical examples to illustrate his view that slavery has actually improved the world. He states that enslaving people is more civil than murdering them, a common practice in what the author refers to as "barbaric" hunting and fishing societies. Having slaves to work in fields led to the great civilizations of the world, Dew argues, and abolishing slavery would be akin to taking a societal step backward.

Without further preliminary, then, we shall advance to the discussion of the question of abolition, noticing not only the plans proposed in the Virginia Legislature, but some others, likewise. And, as the subject of slavery has been considered in every point of view, and pronounced, in the *abstract*, at least, as entirely contrary to the law of nature, we propose taking, in the first place, a hasty view of the origin of slavery, and point out the influence which it has exerted on the progress of civilization. . . .

Thomas R. Dew "Professor Dew on Slavery," in *The Pro-Slavery Argument*. Philadelphia: Lippincott, Grambo & Co, 1853.

Biblical Support of Slavery

Slavery was established and sanctioned by divine authority, among even the elect of heaven, the favored children of Israel. Abraham, the founder of this interesting nation, and the chosen servant of the Lord, was the owner of *hundreds* of slaves. That magnificent shrine, the Temple of Solomon, was reared by the hands of slaves. Egypt's venerable and enduring piles were reared by similar hands. Slavery existed in Assyria and Babylon. The ten tribes of Israel were carried off in bondage to the former by [the Assyrian king] Shalmanezar, and the two tribes of Judah were subsequently carried in triumph by [the Babylonian king] Nebuchadnezzar, to beautify and adorn the latter. Ancient Phoenicia and Carthage had slaves. The Greeks and Trojans, at the siege of Troy, had slaves. Athens, and Sparta, and Thebes, indeed the whole Grecian and Roman worlds, had more slaves than freemen. And in those ages which succeeded the extinction of the Roman empire in the West, "*servi*, or slaves," says Dr. Robertson, "seem to have been the most numerous class." Even in this day of civilization, and the regeneration of governments, slavery is far from being confined to our hemisphere alone. The serf and labor rents prevalent throughout the whole of Eastern Europe, and a portion of Western Asia, and the ryot rents throughout the extensive and over populated countries of the East, and over the dominions of the Porte in Europe, Asia and Africa, but too conclusively mark the existence of slavery over these boundless regions. And when we turn to the continent of Africa, we find slavery, in all its most horrid forms, existing throughout its whole extent, the slaves being at least three times more numerous than the freemen; so that, looking to the whole world, we may, even now, with confidence assert, that slaves, or those whose condition is infinitely worse, form by far the largest portion of the human race. . . .

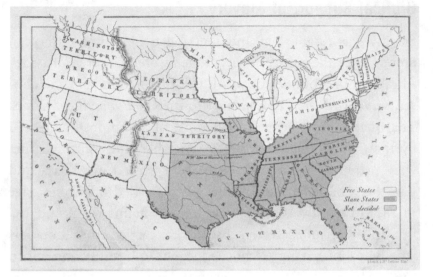

An 1857 map of the United States shows the regions of the country that were "free states," "slave states," and "undecided." Getty Images.

Men as Hunters

Writers on the progress of society designate three stages in which man has been found to exist. First, the hunting or fishing state; second, the pastoral; third, agricultural. Man, in the hunting state, has ever been found to wage war in the most cruel and implacable manner, extermination being the object of the belligerent tribes. Never has there been a finer field presented to the philosopher, for a complete investigation of the character of any portion of our species, than the whole American hemisphere presented, for the complete investigation of the character of savages, in the hunting and fishing state. . . .

Hunting and fishing afford, at best, a very precarious subsistence. Throughout the extensive regions of America, population was found to be most sparsely settled; but, thin as it was, it was most wretchedly and scantily supplied with provisions. Under these circumstances, prisoners of war could not be kept, for the feeding of them would be sure to produce a famine. They would not be sent back to their tribe, for that would strengthen the enemy. They could not even make slaves of them, for their labor would have been worthless. Death, then, was, unfortunately, the punishment, which was prompted both by interest and revenge. And, accordingly, throughout the whole continent of America, we find, with but one or two exceptions, that this was the dreadful fate which awaited the prisoners of all classes, men, women and children. . . .

Slavery Prevents Murder

What is there, let us ask, which is calculated to arrest this horrid practice, and to communicate an impulse towards civilization? Strange as it may sound in modern ears, it is the institution of property and the existence of slavery. Judging from the universality of the fact, we may assert that domestic slavery seems to be the only means of fixing the wanderer to the soil, moderating his savage temper, mitigating the horrors of war, and abolishing the practice of murdering the captives. . . .

So soon as the private right to property is established, slavery commences; and with the institution of slavery, the cruelties of war begin to diminish. The chief finds it to his interest to make slaves of his captives, rather than put them to death. This system commences with the shepherd state, and is consummated in the agricultural. Slavery, therefore, seems to be the chief means of mitigating the horrors of war. Accordingly, wherever, among barbarous nations, they have so far advanced in civilization as to understand the use which may be made of captives, by converting them into slaves, there the cruelties of war are found to be lessened! . . .

In looking to the history of the world, we find that interest, and *interest* alone, has been enabled successfully to war against the fiercer passion of revenge. The only instance of mildness in war, among the savages of North America, results from the operation of interest. Sometimes, when the tribe has suffered great loss of numbers, and stands very much in need of recruits, the prisoner is saved, and adopted as a member of the nation. Pastoral nations require but few slaves, and, consequently, they save but few prisoners for this purpose. Agricultural require more, and this state is the most advantageous to slavery. Prisoners of war are generally spared by such nations, in consideration of the use which may be made of their labor. . . .

The barbarians who overran the Roman Empire existed principally in the pastoral state. They brought along with them their wives and children, and consequently they required extensive regions for their support, and but few slaves. We find, accordingly, they waged a most cruel, exterminating war, not even sparing women and children. . . .

Slavery Rooted in Civilized Society

In after times, during the glorious days of the republics of both Greece and Rome, the wants of man had undergone an enlargement; agriculture had been pushed to a high state of improvement, population became more dense, and consequently a more abundant production, and more regular and constant application of labor, became necessary. At this period, slaves were in great demand, and, therefore, the prisoners of war were generally spared, in order that they might be made slaves. And this mildness did not arise so much from their civilization, as from the great demand for slaves. All the Roman generals, even the mild Julius, were sufficiently cruel to put to death, when they did not choose to make slaves of the captives. Hence, as cruel as were the Greeks and Romans in war, they were much milder than the surrounding barbarous nations. In like manner, the wars in Africa have been made, perhaps, more mild by the *slave trade* than they would otherwise have been. . . .

Let us now close this head, by an inquiry into the justice of slavery, flowing from the laws of war. And here we may observe, in the first place, that the whole of the ancient world, and all nations of modern times verging on a state of barbarism, never for a moment doubted this right. All history proves that they looked upon slavery as a mild punishment, in comparison with what they had a right to inflict. And, so far from being conscience-stricken, when they inflicted the punishment of death or slavery, they seemed to glory in the severity of the punishment, and to be remorseful only when, from some cause, they had not inflicted the worst.

A Rejection of the Pro-Slavery Argument

William Jay

Son of Founding Father John Jay, William Jay worked as a jurist in New York City and published dozens of writings during his life. The best-known of Jay's works was a two-volume account of his father's life. As a member and corresponding foreign secretary of the American Anti-Slavery Society, Jay worked to educate people on the ills of slavery. In this article, Jay examines the comments that Professor Thomas R. Dew made in response to the Virginia State Legislature's debate over the abolition of slavery in 1831. While Dew believes that historical slavery made civil society possible and that it should continue as it has for generations, Jay points out the flaws in the professor's logic. Jay contends that were Dew's points valid, the professor himself would more likely be working in a field than teaching a classroom full of students.

The massacre at Southampton in 1831 [where a group of eight slaves started a revolt that grew to sixty to seventy slaves, who collectively killed fifty-eight white people—hundreds of blacks were later killed in revenge] naturally directed public attention in Virginia, to the danger and consequences of servile insurrections. In the succeeding legislature, a portion of the members were led by the recent tragedy, to suggest the expediency of extinguishing slavery in the State at some distant period, and to propose plans for effecting this object. But the love of power and gain, prevailed over the fear of revolt. Not only was every plan for the abolition of slavery rejected, but an act was passed which its authors believed would give additional permanency and security to the institution. A

William Jay, "Remarks on Professor Dew's Vindication of Perpetual Slavery," *The Quarterly Anti-Slavery Magazine*, April 1836, pp. 211–225.

large appropriation was made for the transportation of free negroes to Africa; and lest masters should occasionally avail themselves of this mode of getting rid of their slaves, and thus give an impulse to emancipation, it was expressly provided, that no slave to be thereafter emancipated should have the benefit of the appropriation.

Slave Rebellion Raises Concern

Such a result to the deliberations of a legislature convened immediately after the most appalling servile insurrection recorded in our annals, might, we should think, have satisfied the most devoted partisan of slavery. The debates were published, and they disclosed the alarming fact, that there were native Virginians, men of character and influence, who believed slavery to be a moral and political evil which ought to be removed at some future day. It was important to the permanency of the institution, that this dangerous heresy should be at once assailed and vanquished, and Mr. Thomas R. Dew, Professor of History, Metaphysics and Political Law, in William and Mary College, immediately buckled on his armor, and sallied forth a champion for the true faith. And never did a knight-errant exhibit a more gallant bearing; nor did even the hero of La Mancha, rush upon the windmills with more reckless intrepidity, than does our chivalric Professor battle with history and experience, and reason, and the moral sense of mankind. Such courage cannot but excite our admiration, while the courtesy that adorns it, claims our acknowledgments. Accustomed as we are to the rude demeanor of our northern advocates of slavery, as well as to their pusillanimity in admitting its sinfulness, while they justify its continuance, it is really pleasing to meet a champion of interminable bondage, who is at once, a hero and a gentleman.

It is a little unlucky for the Professor, that he descended into the arena so early as 1832, since his first thrust is at the folly of those Virginians who think and talk about the abolition of slavery, whereas "the Parliament of Great Britain with all its philanthropic zeal, guided by the wisdom and eloquence of such statesmen as [Lord] Chatham, [James] Fox, [Edmund] Burke, [William] Pitt, [George] Canning and [Lord Henry] *Brougham*, has never yet seriously agitated this question in regard to their West India possessions." Now it so happens that only two years after this compliment to the British Parliament at the expense of Virginia legislators, that same body, influenced in part by the efforts of Brougham, decreed that within six years slavery should cease throughout the empire; and that personal rights, and civil and religious privileges, should no longer depend upon "the tincture of a skin."

Our author now enters upon the defence of slavery, and satisfactorily proves that it is not a modern institution. Indeed he traces it to very high antiquity, and shews that it has prevailed over a large portion of the globe. In these respects, however, it must yield the palm to murder, since the latter crime dates its commencement in the family of Adam, and has been more or less perpetrated among every people from the time of Cain to the present hour. . . .

Dew Defends Slavery as an Alternative to Murder

Under this head we are treated with a fervid description of the horrors of savage warfare, and in contemplating the awful picture his own pencil had drawn, Mr. Dew exclaims, "what is there, let us ask, which is calculated to arrest this horrid practice, (killing and eating prisoners of war,) and to communicate an impulse towards civilization? Strange as it may sound in modern ears, it is the institution of property, and the existence of slavery." With all his boldness, our champion just at this stage of the combat, seems to draw a quicker breath than usual. He talks of "the institution of property, *and* the existence of slavery," when he evidently means the institution of property *in* human beings. It is no reason why a savage warrior should not kill and eat his prisoner, because he possesses a horse; but a very sufficient one, if that prisoner can be converted like the horse into a beast of burthen for his captor's service.

Savage warfare then, is one source of slavery—let us see *how* the source sanctifies the stream. "Judging from the universality of the fact we may assert that domestic slavery seems the ONLY means of fixing the wanderer to the soil, moderating his savage temper, mitigating the horrors of war, and abolishing the practice of murdering the captives."

We commend this new plan for effecting civilization, to our missionary boards, and suggest to them the expediency of instructing their missionaries in savage countries, to direct all their efforts in the first instance, to the establishment of domestic slavery, as preparatory to the introduction of the Gospel. Should the missionaries, or their employers have any scruples of conscience about reducing prisoners of war to servitude, let them attend to the following argument:—"The whole of the ancient world, and all nations of modern times *verging on a state of barbarism* never for a moment doubted this right. All history proves that they have looked upon slavery as a mild punishment in comparison with what they had a right to inflict; and so far from being conscience stricken when they inflicted the punishment of death or slavery, they seemed to glory in the severity of the punishment."

History Does Not Defend Slavery

We are next taught, that the great men of antiquity had none of the modern fastidiousness, on the subject of slavery, and the instances given to prove this point, furnish us, accidentally as it would seem, with the following beautiful illustration of the civilizing, humanizing influence of the practice of enslaving prisoners of war. "Julius Cæsar has been reckoned one of the mildest and most clement military chieftains of antiquity, and yet there is very little doubt that the principal object in the invasion of Britain was to procure slaves for the Roman markets. When he left Britain, it became necessary to collect together *a large fleet* for the purpose of transporting his captives across the channel. He sometimes ordered the captive chiefs to be executed, and he butchered the whole of Cato's Senate, when he became master of Utica. Paulus Emilius [a Roman consul] acting under the special orders of the Roman Senate, laid all Epirus waste, and brought 150,000 captives in chains to Italy, all of whom were sold in the Roman slave-markets."

Thus it would seem that the invasion of Britain, and the devastation of Epirus were caused by the influence of slavery, and that although Cæsar was so distinguished a patron of this humanizing institution, he could nevertheless slaughter not only captive chiefs, but even the whole Utica Senate.

But to proceed—"If we turn from profane history to Holy Writ, that sacred fountain whence are derived those pure precepts and holy laws and regulations by which the Christian world has ever been governed, we shall find that the children of Israel under the guidance of Jehovah, massacred or enslaved their prisoners of war." When the Creator and Almighty Governor of the Universe shall devote the British nation to destruction for their sins, and shall by a series of stupendous miracles, require and enable the southern planters to execute his wrath, they will no doubt be excusable in killing or enslaving as many Englishmen as possible; but it is not clear to us, that in an ordinary war, the rights of victors over their prisoners, are thus extensive. The Professor indeed, does not explicitly contend for this right as belonging to *civilized* belligerents, but seems chiefly to rely on the *rights of savage* warriors, to make out his first source of slavery. Now it will be recollected, that it is part of the very essence of slavery, that it is perpetuated by descent. Let us suppose that one of the ancestors of our Virginia Professor had been captured by the royal but savage father of Pocahontas, and had, after the peace effected by that generous damsel, been sold as a slave to one of the Colonists. The whole transaction, according to the teacher of "Political Law" in William and Mary College, would have been strictly legal, sanctioned not only by innumerable instances in savage warfare, but by the example of Julius Cæsar, Paulus Emilius, and other great men of antiquity, and above all, by the conduct of "the children of Israel under the guidance of Jehovah." The posterity of the hapless captive, would of course through successive generations have been lawfully held in bondage, and the Professor, instead of publishing theories about slavery, would at the present day, by his own shewing, be fairly, justly and honestly experiencing in his own person the blessings of hopeless interminable servitude, with the assurance that his own fate would be the inheritance of his children after him.

Lincoln's Emancipation Proclamation

Abraham Lincoln

President Abraham Lincoln is remembered today as the "Great Emancipator," but the sixteenth president fought a long and hard battle to free the slaves of the United States. Early in his presidency, Lincoln proposed the gradual emancipation of slaves throughout the country. The president found little support for this idea in the legislature. After several states seceded from the Union, Lincoln made the following proclamation. It states that all slaves living in rebellious states will be freed unless the states rejoin the Union. Lincoln hoped that this proclamation would end the conflict peacefully, but the war continued. However, many historians and scholars view Lincoln's proclamation as the groundwork for the Thirteenth Amendment.

Whereas, on the twenty-second day of September, in the year of our Lord one thousand eight hundred and sixty-two, a proclamation was issued by the President of the United States, containing, among other things, the following, to wit:

"That on the first day of January, in the year of our Lord one thousand eight hundred and sixty-three, all persons held as slaves within any State or designated part of a State, the people whereof shall then be in rebellion against the United States, shall be then, thenceforward, and forever free; and the Executive Government of the United States, including the military and naval authority thereof, will recognize and maintain the freedom of such persons, and will do no act or acts to repress such persons, or any of them, in any efforts they may make for their actual freedom.

"That the Executive will, on the first day of January aforesaid, by proclamation, designate the States and parts of States,

Abraham Lincoln, "The Emancipation Proclamation," January 1, 1863.

The first reading of the Emancipation Proclamation before President Lincoln's cabinet in 1866. Photo Researchers, Inc.

if any, in which the people thereof, respectively, shall then be in rebellion against the United States; and the fact that any State, or the people thereof, shall on that day be, in good faith, represented in the Congress of the United States by members chosen thereto at elections wherein a majority of the qualified voters of such State shall have participated, shall, in the absence of strong countervailing testimony, be deemed conclusive evidence that such State, and the people thereof, are not then in rebellion against the United States."

Now, therefore I, Abraham Lincoln, President of the United States, by virtue of the power in me vested as Commander-in-Chief, of the Army and Navy of the United States in time of actual armed rebellion against the authority and government of the United States, and as a fit and necessary war measure for suppressing said rebellion, do, on this first day of January, in the year of our Lord one thousand eight hundred and sixty-three, and in accordance with my purpose so to do publicly proclaimed for the full period of one hundred days, from the day first above mentioned, order and designate as the States and parts of States wherein the people thereof respectively, are this day in rebellion against the United States, the following, to wit:

Arkansas, Texas, Louisiana, (except the Parishes of St. Bernard, Plaquemines, Jefferson, St. John, St. Charles, St. James Ascension, Assumption, Terrebonne, Lafourche, St. Mary, St. Martin, and Orleans, including the City of New Orleans) Mississippi, Alabama, Florida, Georgia, South Carolina, North Carolina, and Virginia, (except the forty-eight counties designated as West Virginia, and also the counties of Berkley, Accomac, Northampton, Elizabeth City, York, Princess Ann, and Norfolk, including the cities of Norfolk and Portsmouth[)], and which excepted parts, are for the present, left precisely as if this proclamation were not issued.

And by virtue of the power, and for the purpose aforesaid, I do order and declare that all persons held as slaves within said designated States, and parts of States, are, and henceforward shall be free; and that the Executive government of the United States, including the military and naval authorities thereof, will recognize and maintain the freedom of said persons.

And I hereby enjoin upon the people so declared to be free to abstain from all violence, unless in necessary self-defence; and I recommend to them that, in all cases when allowed, they labor faithfully for reasonable wages.

And I further declare and make known, that such persons of suitable condition, will be received into the armed service of the United States to garrison forts, positions, stations, and other places, and to man vessels of all sorts in said service.

And upon this act, sincerely believed to be an act of justice, warranted by the Constitution, upon military necessity, I invoke the considerate judgment of mankind, and the gracious favor of Almighty God.

In witness whereof, I have hereunto set my hand and caused the seal of the United States to be affixed.

Done at the City of Washington, this first day of January, in the year of our Lord one thousand eight hundred and sixty three, and of the Independence of the United States of America the eighty-seventh.

Questioning the Proclamation

The New York Times

In response to Abraham Lincoln's Emancipation Proclamation, the New York Times *published an editorial examining the motives of the president and the possible repercussions of his actions. The author argues that the proclamation has nothing to do with the issue of abolishing slavery but is really a political maneuver to urge the rebellious states to rejoin the Union without any more bloodshed. The article points out that no slaves were freed by the president's proclamation and that many wondered whether Lincoln would be forced to revoke it altogether. The author examines all of the concerns and thoughts of the people of the day. At first he questions whether the proclamation is a complete failure, as it will do little to help free slaves residing in rebellious states. Then he points out the disadvantage that these states will face if forced to wage war without slaves to help them.*

The President's Proclamation

We find it utterly impossible to account, on any just principles, for the hostility evinced in Democratic quarters to the President's Proclamation menacing the rebels with emancipation of their slaves unless they return to their allegiance. It is a purely military proceeding—aiming at the overthrow of the rebellion and the restoration of the Union. If its object were the abolition of Slavery, it would have decreed that abolition, as it might have done under the law of Congress, at once, and as a penalty for past offences. But it does nothing of the sort. It merely gives the rebels notice that, if they persist in rebellion beyond a certain time, their slaves shall be set free. It is precisely such a notice as is sent to a besieged town—that unless they surrender by a fixed date their town will be bombarded.

The New York Times, The President's Proclamation, November 12, 1862, p. 4.

The Problem with the Proclamation

Not a single slave has yet been set free by this Proclamation. The rebels have it in their power to prevent the liberation of a single slave under its provisions—and that, too, without doing anything but what it is their duty to do under any circumstances. They claim—or their Northern sympathizers claim for them—the guarantees of the Constitution. Let them return to its shelter and they will have the full benefit of them. They have repudiated its obligations,—why should they be entitled to its protection? The moment they acknowledge its authority they will receive all the protection which that authority carries with it. The fate of Slavery is thus exclusively in their own hands. If they seek its abolition, they can secure it. If they desire its preservation, they can secure that.

But it is claimed that they ought not to be thus compelled to choose between Slavery and Secession, but that they should be allowed to enjoy both—that the National Government should protect the former for them while they are waging war upon it to secure the latter. The mere statement of the claim proves its absurdity. No community can have War and Peace at the same time. If they choose to wage war they must surrender for the time the blessings and securities of peace. We of the North are compelled to make a similar choice. We surrender the lives of our sons, millions of property, the prosperity of peaceful industry, possibly the security of our homes, because we deem a war for the Union worth all these sacrifices. The South in the same way must hold its property and its peace subject to the chances of war, if it is determined to wage war. So long as it fights against the Government it has no claim to its protection or forbearance.

Nor is there the shadow of a reason why Slavery should claim exemption from the rigors and exposures which war brings upon all other forms of property and of labor. There is nothing in the Constitution which guarantees to it such exemption. True, that instrument provides that no man shall be "deprived of life, liberty or property, but by due process of law." But this does not secure the slaveholding rebel in the possession of his *slave*, any more than of his cattle, his musket or his life. If the latter may be taken to war, so may the former. And if the Government can make war at all for the preservation of its integrity, it must hold the life, liberty and property of its enemies subject to the chances and necessities of war. And it has precisely the same right to confiscate and liberate the slaves of rebels, as a means of prosecuting the war and making it effective, which it has to seize their property or imprison their persons.

But it is urged that this measure tends to incite *insurrection* among the slaves, and thus to involve the innocent in destruction. Whose duty is it to protect them against such calamities? Whose duty is it to keep the slaves in subjection and to guard the women and children of the slave plantations against their violence? Clearly that of the slave-owners themselves. If they are unable to do this, and call on the General Government, through their State authorities, to aid them in it, it is the duty of that Government to give them that aid,—but only when they acknowledge its authority, and on the basis of that acknowledgement claim its protection. But there is no pretence here that they are *unable* to prevent or suppress insurrections. They have their whole population under arms. They can turn the whole power of their armies against their slaves at an hour's notice, and thus render revolt impossible. Why do they not do this? Because they want to employ their troops against us! And they expect us to keep or leave their slaves in subjection, so that they may be free to do so! We must not touch their slaves, lest we should thus put them under the necessity of using their troops elsewhere than against us. That seems to us an absolutely conclusive argument on the other side.

What Were They Really Fighting For?

With the exception of a very few Abolitionists, nobody at the North was ever in favor of waging war upon the South for the purpose of freeing its slaves. The great body of the Republicans, as of every other party at the North, would to-day oppose a war waged for such a purpose. President Lincoln would be the last man living to commence such a war, or give it his support. The war is waged now, as it has been from the beginning, *to crush the rebellion and restore the Union and the supremacy of the Constitution.* This is its sole and exclusive object. But against the attainment of that object, Slavery proves to be a formidable and, apparently, a fatal obstacle. It is felt and seen to be the main strength of the rebellion. It is the basis on which it rests. Instead of being, as we had supposed it would be, an element of weakness to the South in war, it supplies them with food, with labor, with all the home comforts they require, and thus sends to the field the whole fighting population of the Southern States. There is no law of Nations, of the Constitution, or of common sense, which requires or permits us to leave so powerful a weapon in the hands of our enemies, untouched. It is our duty, if we seek success, to wrest it from their hands, or to paralyze it in their grasp.

Democratic orators and journalists are speculating largely on the probability that President Lincoln will revoke this proclamation, or fail to fulfill the menace which it involves. Why they should desire him to do so they have not yet made clear. If they regard Slavery as of more value than the Union—if they prefer that the Government should perish rather than Slavery be disturbed—their action is natural and easily understood. But they have hitherto always disclaimed such a preference. They profess a desire to see the war prosecuted with vigor, and the rebellion crushed. If they are sincere in these professions, they cannot object to emancipation as a legitimate weapon for the accomplishment of these ends.

A Defense of the Proclamation

Allen C. Guelzo

In the weeks and months following the announcement of Abraham Lincoln's Emancipation Proclamation, the president faced sharp criticism from political figures both inside and outside his party. Many argued that Lincoln was selfishly turning the war for the Union into a battle for abolition. After receiving an invitation to a meeting of Republicans in his home state of Illinois, Lincoln, unable to attend, resolved to use the meeting as an opportunity to address people's concerns over emancipation. In a letter, read at the meeting by James Cook Conkling, Lincoln gives his strongest defense of his proclamation. The president asks his critics to think about how history will judge them for their hesitation to endorse emancipation. He also urges those concerned solely with preserving the Union to see the practical benefits of freeing slaves in rebellious states. The author of the following viewpoint, Allen C. Guelzo, describes this letter as one of the best examples of Lincoln's political genius. Guelzo also contends that a direct line can be drawn from the Emancipation Proclamation to the Conkling letter to the Thirteenth Amendment. Guelzo is a professor at Gettysburg College, where he is the director of the Civil War era studies program.

A braham Lincoln might well have believed that "I never in my life was more certain that I was doing right than I do in signing" the Emancipation Proclamation into military law on January 1, 1863. But doing what was right and what was politically viable were two different things. "At no time during the war was the depression among the people of the North so great as in the spring of 1863," remembered [congressman] James G. Blaine, and largely because "the anti-slavery policy of the President was . . . tending to a fatal division among the

Allen C. Guelzo, "Defending Emancipation: Abraham Lincoln and the Conkling Letter," *Civil War History*, vol. 48, no. 4, December 2002, pp. 313–339.

people." The simple fact of announcing his intention to proclaim emancipation back in September had created more public anger than Lincoln had anticipated. William O. Stoddard, one of Lincoln's White House staffers, gloomily recalled

> how many editors and how many other penmen within these past few days rose in anger to remind Lincoln that this is a war for the Union only, and they never gave him any authority to run it as an Abolition war. They never, never told him that he might set the negroes free, and, now that he has done so, or futilely pretended to do so, he is a more unconstitutional tyrant and a more odious dictator than ever he was before. They tell him, however, that his edict, his ukase, his decree, his firman, his venomous blow at the sacred liberty of white men to own black men is mere brutem fulmen, and a dead letter and a poison which will not work. They tell him many other things, and, among them, they tell him that the army will fight no more, and that the hosts of the Union will indignantly disband rather than be sacrificed upon the bloody altar of fanatical Abolitionism.

Reaction to the Emancipation Proclamation

It was not that Lincoln or the Proclamation lacked defenders. A long queue of prominent Republicans—George Boker, Francis Lieber, Grosvenor Lowrey, and Robert Dale Owen—promptly entered the lists with pamphlets and articles. But an equally formidable roster of Northern Democratic critics and jurists—including Benjamin Curtis, Montgomery Throop, and Joel Parker—were there waiting for them. Agitation mounted in many places for a negotiated settlement to the war or a national peace convention that would avoid emancipation. "The Darkest hour of our Country's trial is yet to come," warned Benjamin F. Butler. Nothing is surer than an assembly to settle this struggle on the basis of the Union as it was? Even worse, it was rumored "that the President will recoil from his Emancipation Proclamation" because of the heavy political costs it imposed. In the end, if Lincoln had any hope of turning public opinion in favor of emancipation by argument, the arguments would have to be his, and he would have to be his own best apologist for the Proclamation.

The surest mark of how Lincoln rose to that challenge is the public letter he wrote on August 26, 1863, for James Cook Conkling and a "mass meeting of unconditional Union men" in Lincoln's own home town of Springfield, Illinois. After months of uncertainty, the Conkling letter signaled that Lincoln's commitment to emancipation was absolute and would not be bargained away in return for concessions by the Confederates. Thus, a straight line runs from the Proclamation through the Conkling letter to the Thirteenth Amendment and the final abolition of slavery. . . .

The Conkling Connection

James Cook Conkling was, like Lincoln, a Springfield lawyer, and his wife, Mercy Levering, had been a close friend of Mary Todd Lincoln's. Born in New York in 1816 and a graduate of Princeton, Conkling had clerked briefly in New Jersey then moved to Illinois in 1838 and was admitted to the bar that October. Like Lincoln, he had been an ardent Whig and successfully ran for both mayor of Springfield in 1845 and then the state legislature in 1851, where "he was identified with a small group of able men who were prominent in anti-slavery legislation." He joined the Republicans, became a member of the state Republican committee in 1856, but lost a race for the U.S. House. Conkling was one of fifteen Sangamon County delegates to the 1860 state nominating convention in Decatur that pledged itself to Lincoln's nomination for the presidency, and he prided himself on having "voted regularly for Mr. Lincoln for more than a quarter century whenever he aspired to any office." He strongly defended Lincoln's policies, including military arrests. "While the Government is contending against armed traitors it must also crush incipient treason," he icily

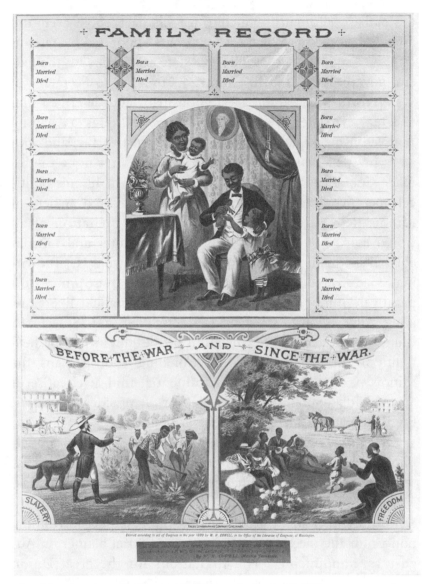

For African Americans, family portraits before and after the Civil War were two vastly different images. Before the war, images included the slave owner. After the war, freed slaves were depicted as more relaxed and at leisure. Corbis. Reproduced by permission.

wrote to one former Democratic acquaintance who had been imprisoned in Fort Warren as a Confederate sympathizer. "It is therefore ... justified in arresting those who refuse to take the oath of allegiance." Lincoln, for his part, spoke well and highly of Conkling. When Conkling was appointed by Yates as Illinois's state agent to oversee the state accounts with the federal government, Lincoln endorsed Conkling to Secretary of War [Edwin M.] Stanton as "a good man" and described him to Quartermaster General Montgomery Meigs as having "ample business qualification, is entirely trustworthy; and with all is my personal friend of long standing." Yet none of this made Conkling much more than an important Illinois political operative. It was revealing of the disarray and anxiety of Illinois Republicans that the most crucial invitation of all would come not from key Illinois party figures and Lincoln allies like Joseph Medill, Leonard Swett, [Orville H.] Browning, Isaac Arnold or "Long John" Wentworth but from a comparatively minor political player from Springfield like Conkling. And yet, just as [Glenn C.] Altschuler and [Stuart M.] Blumin suggested, the organization of the rally would be held tightly in the hands of men like Conkling—not, perhaps, the Illinois party elite but still an influential mid-level cadre of Springfield Republicans who were, for all practical purposes, the Republican leadership of central Illinois.

Given the lack of sponsorship from the great names of Illinois Republicanism, neither Conkling nor his Springfield associates were taking any chances that the "Great Union Mass Meeting" would fall short of the mark set by the June 17 Democratic meeting. The Illinois State Journal began running notices for the meeting under its own editorial banner on August 13, announcing, "The Invitations for the great Union Mass Meeting are nearly all issued and the call with a large number of names appended, will appear in a few days.". . .

On August 14, Conkling extended the invitation to the president, adding reasons why Lincoln should accept:

The unconditional union men in our State are to hold a Grand Mass Meeting at Springfield on the 3rd Day of September next. It would be gratifying to the many thousands who will be present on that occasion if you would also meet with them. . . . A visit to your old home would not be inappropriate if you can break away from the pressure of public duties. We intend to make the most imposing demonstration that has ever been held in the Northwest. Many of the most distinguished men in the country have been, and will be invited to attend and I know that nothing could add more to the interest of the occasion than your presence.

Conkling later explained, "We hardly expected he would be present, but we hoped to receive some communication which would indicate his future policy and give encouragement to his friends." At that moment, however, Conkling was evidently very much in earnest about the possibility of Lincoln's presence in Springfield. . . .

By August 23, Lincoln had decided not to make the journey. Part of the motivation was his anxiety over the uncertain military situation in Virginia and Tennessee, where Lincoln hoped that both Maj. Gen. George G. Meade and Maj. Gen. William S. Rosecrans would pursue the Confederate armies. Part of his reasoning also may have been due to a reluctance to feed the accusations of critics like [Clement Laird] Vallandigham by looking as though, by personal appearance in Springfield, he endorsed [Richard] Yates's unilateral dismissal of the legislature as a good way of dealing with opposition. However, Lincoln could not disengage himself entirely from the Illinois situation, and so he chose instead to write a public letter for Conkling to read to the meeting on his behalf. . . .

Lincoln Responds to His Critics

The letter was Lincoln's most extensive and forthright defense of emancipation since the issuance of the Proclamation itself. The letter, all of 1,662 words long, falls logically into six sections. The first was a simple salutation to Conkling and to the organizers of the meeting, "my old political friends"; but it also made an opening political gesture of recognition to War

Democrats, "those other noble men, whom no partizan malice, or partizan hope, can make false to the nation's life."

That much said, Lincoln plunged bluntly into the second section, where it was clear at once that he intended to speak over the heads of the loyalists at the mass meeting to the very anti-emancipation Democrats who had triggered the legislative rumpus of the past spring, in the evident hope that they might be willing to keep supporting the war if they could have their anger at emancipation reasoned away. "There are those who are dissatisfied with me," he said simply, adding that their dissatisfaction came down to one thing: "You desire peace; and you blame me that we do not have it." What he asked the dissatisfied to do at that point was to reflect on how peace could actually be obtained. "There are but three conceivable ways." First was to keep on with the war and "suppress the rebellion by force of arms. This I am trying to do." Could there be any disagreement with that? "Are you for it?" he asked rhetorically. Lincoln presumed so, but he accepted for the moment that they did not and moved on to suggest a second way to bring peace: "give up the Union." Were there any takers for that? "Are you for it?" This time, he presumed not. In that case, "If you are not for force, nor yet for dissolution, there only remains some imaginable compromise." Could anyone really imagine from where such a Union-saving compromise would come? Not from anyone in the South. "The strength of the rebellion, is its military—its army," Lincoln explained, and the Rebel military showed no inclination at all to compromise. Even if the Confederate politicians in Richmond would announce their interest in negotiations, "no paper compromise, to which the controllers of [General Robert E.] Lee's army are not agreed, can, at all, affect that army," and "no word or intimation, from that rebel army, or from any of the men controlling it, in relation to any peace compromise, has ever come to my knowledge of belief." Moreover, any efforts by well-intentioned Northerners to propose an armistice would only "waste time, which the enemy would improve to our disadvantage; and that would be all." There was, in other words, no way forward for saving the Union except to fight determinedly and unitedly to victory over the Confederacy. All the wild talk of national peace conventions weakened that resolve.

Lincoln understood that this was not the real grounds for the "dissatisfaction," or even the calls for national compromise. He began the third section of the letter with an accusation: "But, to be plain, you are dissatisfied with me about the negro." Indeed they were, and he knew that this "difference of opinion between you and myself upon that subject" was the issue before which all the other dissatisfactions were little more than smoke-screens. Lincoln's gambit was to seize the moral high ground, and turn the debate from a vicious argument about race to a more imposing argument about the Union. "I certainly wish that all men could be free," Lincoln wrote, which was an assertion so disarming that no one could easily object—and knowing that the president turned the knife deftly on his critics by adding, "while I suppose you do not." Having cast them neatly to the disadvantage, Lincoln still protested that he did not propose to make even that an issue: "Yet I have neither adopted, nor proposed any measure, which is not consistent with even your view." He then added the proviso that would be crucial to the entire development of his argument: "provided you are for the Union." The strategy of the letter was now becoming apparent. By establishing a common commitment to saving the Union as paramount, Lincoln was now ready (after the irresistible suggestion that the anti-emancipation Democrats had put their party over the last six months in the place of denouncing both union and freedom) to ask whether any of his emancipation polices had been anything else except services to the cause of the Union. . . .

A counterargument lurked here that the Proclamation was so radical a gesture that it was the principal reason why the

Union was becoming impossible to restore. "Some of you profess to think its retraction would operate favorably for the Union." But practically speaking, the truth was that "the war has certainly progressed as favorably for us, since the issue of the proclamation as before." (Corollary: if really you are for the Union, there is no reason to retract the Emancipation Proclamation). The irony of these protests, Lincoln pointed out, is that all the while "you say you will not fight to free negroes," there were large numbers of emancipated blacks who "seem willing to fight for you." Everyone of them who is willing to subtract himself or herself from the Confederate warmaking effort by running away to the Union lines, or who is willing to don a Union uniform and carry a rifle against the Rebels, is providing just so much more aid in saving the Union. "I thought that in your struggle for the Union, to whatever extent the negroes should cease helping the enemy, to that extent it weakened the enemy in his resistance to you. Do you think differently?" Lincoln again jabbed rhetorically. . . .

Lincoln would grant this much to his political critics. If they wished "exclusively to save the Union" and not to emancipate slaves, their love for the Union (if really you are for the Union) was quite acceptable and should carry them forward with him to the goal of saving it. "Fight you, then, exclusively to save the Union," the president encouraged. Whenever they had succeeded in conquering "all resistance to the Union," if Lincoln should ask them to fight any longer after that, then "it will be an apt time, then, for you to declare you will not fight to free negroes." All this, of course, was a highly subtle joke. By the time such critics had fought and saved the Union, the war for black freedom would also be over. But while the war was still on, there was no other way to get black help to save the Union than through offering blacks freedom. "Negroes, like other people, act upon motives." If, for the sake of saving the Union, "they stake their lives for us, they must be prompted by the strongest motive—even the promise of freedom." Here, Lincoln added ominously, "the promise being made, must be kept." There would, in other words, be no taking back of the Emancipation Proclamation. A pledge of life had to be balanced with a pledge of freedom, a pledge so solemn that it would balance forever the risk of life.

Saving the Union

Then, abruptly, the argument for emancipation seemed spent. Lincoln turned quickly and briefly in the fourth section of the letter to what many at the fairgrounds might have imagined would have been the longer subject of his letter, a review of the progress of the war. "The signs look better." The Mississippi was now open with the fall of Vicksburg, and the "Father of Waters again goes unvexed to the sea." The northwest and the northeast had all contributed their strength, and so even had the unionist South, "in black and white." Victories at "Antietam, Murfreesboro, Gettysburg, and on many fields of lesser note" had been won, while the navy—"Uncle Sam's Web-feet"—had imposed a blockade that covered the deep sea as well as "wherever the ground was a little damp." Thanks went to all, "For the great republic—for the principle it lives by, and keeps alive—for man's great future,—thanks to all."

Lincoln had one more round to fire on behalf of emancipation in the fifth and most acerbic section. "Peace does not appear so distant as it did," he concluded, and when it did, the peace would prove the basic point he had been struggling to make since his July 4, 1861, special message to Congress: "that among free men, there can be no successful appeal from the ballot to the bullet," that in democracies, minorities cannot willfully destroy a polity because they have not triumphed, and still pretend that they are functioning democratically. When that case is proved—and if really Democrats really were for the Union—then it will be discovered that "there will be some black men who can remember that, with silent tongue, and clenched teeth, and steady eye, and well-poised bayonet, they have helped mankind on to this great consummation." What, then, would the critics have to say to such men, who had helped them make their own case for the Union and democracy? "While, I fear," Lincoln continued, "there will be some white ones, unable to forget that, with malignant heart, and deceitful speech, they have strove to hinder it." If any of them happened to have been sitting in the Illinois legislature that spring, they knew now what conclusions Lincoln expected them to draw about their own role in history.

Arguments over Amendment XIII

George William Curtis

In December 1863 several members of Congress proposed bills that would change the Constitution and abolish slavery in the United States. After drafts of the proposed amendment had been written, voting began in both houses of Congress. While the bill for the proposed Thirteenth Amendment failed to pass in the House of Representatives, it won the support of the Senate in April 1864. Only six senators voted against the amendment. In this article, the Harper's Weekly *editor George William Curtis gives his thoughts on the speeches of four of the dissenters. He finds each of the men's arguments wholly unsupportable. More important, the editor explains why it is necessary for the bill to become law so that those who gave their lives for the Union will not have done so in vain and so that the survivors of the country's great divide can finally heal. In addition to serving as political editor for* Harper's Weekly, *Curtis was a writer and an orator.*

On the 8th of April, 1864, at the close of the third year of a civil war produced by the tragical and futile effort to unite in one peaceful government the principle of the fullest popular freedom and of the most abject despotism, the Senate of the United States, by a vote of thirty-eight to six, proposed to amend the Constitution in the manner itself provides, for the purpose of prohibiting slavery in the United States. That nothing might be wanting to the moral grandeur and dignity of the occasion, the resistance offered to this truly American act by the truly un-American advocates of human slavery was as contemptible as the system itself is revolting.

George William Curtis, *Harper's Weekly*, April 23, 1864. Retrieved March 1, 2008, from http://13thamendment.harpweek.com/.

The Dissenters' Arguments

Of the six Senators who voted against the resolution four made brief speeches. Mr. [Lazarus Whitehead] *Powell*, of Kentucky, said that if there had been no Abolitionists there would have been no rebellion: an inanity too incredible. Mr. [William] *Saulsbury*, of Delaware, proposed to secure liberty of speech and of the press, and re-establish the principles of the Missouri Compromise—which was a proposition to feed a fire with water. For how can slavery and free speech coexist? Mr. [Garrett]*Davis*, of Kentucky, declared the constitutional abolition of slavery a wicked and unjust act, against which he was aware the protest of an angel would be of no avail; forgetting that the only angel who would have wished to protest was named *Lucifer*, and fell from heaven. Mr. [James A.] *M'Dougall*, of California, announced that he was devoted to human freedom, and therefore, as a true friend of man, should vote in favor of slavery.

And this was the expiring gasp in the United States Senate of the infernal iniquity to whose service the clear, cold casuistry and subtle sophistry of *Calhoun* was formerly devoted; before which *Webster* used to bow; from whose snare the human-hearted *Clay* could never break away; which, by the universal obsequiousness of the American people, had succeeded in coiling its horrid folds around all our liberties, and from whose fatal embrace this war is the struggle of the national life to escape. Yet that final escape is worth the war. The innumerable hearts that are broken, the countless homes that are desolate in our own land, and the earnest friends in other countries who understand the scope of the struggle, will own that when the great act initiated by the Senate is completed, the costly sacrifice of youth and hope and love is not in vain, and that the future of equal justice which this measure secures is well bought by all the blood and sorrow of the war.

The issue is at last openly joined. If the House fail to concur by the necessary two-thirds vote, the Congressional elections of next autumn will turn upon the question of the Constitutional Amendment, and the vote of this spring shows what the result will be.

CONSTITUTIONAL
AMENDMENTS
BEYOND THE BILL OF RIGHTS

CHAPTER 2

Cases Concerning the Thirteenth Amendment

Early Supreme Court Rulings Undermine Amendment XIII

Douglas L. Colbert

Douglas L. Colbert, in his 1995 article "Liberating the Thirteenth Amendment," discusses the Thirteenth Amendment and the legal decisions that have affected it throughout the years. In this excerpt Colbert specifically describes how early Supreme Court rulings regarding the Thirteenth Amendment worked to undermine the authority and power of the amendment. Colbert describes how the Thirteenth Amendment severely suffered from the narrow interpretation of the Constitution and the views and biases of the justices in such decisions as those in the Slaughter-House Cases *and* Plessy v. Ferguson. *These decisions, according to Colbert, also stripped Congress of any power to enforce the Thirteenth Amendment, rendering the amendment powerless against social and racial injustices. Colbert is a professor of law at Maryland School of Law.*

Supreme Court decisions between 1872 and 1876 laid the foundation for the Court's "counterrevolution" against Reconstruction federalism. This counterrevolution culminated in 1883 in the *Civil Right Cases* [a group of five similar cases consolidated into one issue for the Supreme Court to review. The Court held that the enforcement provision or the Fourteenth Amendment—to outlaw racial discrimination by private Individuals and Organizations—was beyond the scope of Congressional authority.], in which the Court's view of the Thirteenth Amendment shifted back to a pre-Reconstruction concept of federalism, requiring the national government to defer to local governments' enforcement of civil rights laws. Thirteen years later in *Plessy v. Ferguson,* the Court delivered

Douglas L. Colbert, "Liberating the Thirteenth Amendment," *Harvard Civil Rights-Civil Liberties Law Review*, vol. 30, Winter 1995, pp. 17, 19–21, 25–28. Copyright © 1995 by Harvard Civil Rights-Civil Liberties Law Review. Reproduced by permission.

another devastating blow to the Thirteenth Amendment, rendering it obsolete except in situations involving compulsory exploitation of labor and peonage [involuntary servitude].

Supreme Court Decisions 1872–1876

The evolution of Thirteenth Amendment jurisprudence, from the badges-of-slavery analysis to the narrow interpretations that defeated the Amendment's original purpose and confined it for the next 100 years, began with *Blyew v. United States*. Even though the Court's decision upheld the 1866 Act's [the 1886 Act gives jurisdiction to the circuit court of all cases involving people who are denied or cannot enforce in state or local courts the rights given to them under the act] constitutionality, it reversed the defendants' federal convictions and undermined federal civil rights removal jurisdiction. Despite the *Blyew* Court's remarkably tortured reasoning, the decision endured to restrict severely the use of federal removal prosecutions in instances when states failed to protect African American victims of racially motivated violence. . . .

The *Blyew* decision illustrates how the Supreme Court defeated Congress's attempt to eliminate one of slavery's primary badges by narrowly interpreting the 1866 Act's removal provision. *Blyew* initiated the judicial retreat from the Reconstruction goal of liberating African Americans from slavery and inferior citizenship status.

The Supreme Court continued this retreat in *United States v. Cruikshank*. In *Cruikshank*, the Supreme Court upheld the reversal of conspiracy convictions against three Ku Klux Klan defendants in "[t]he bloodiest single instance of racial carnage in the Reconstruction era." In dismissing the indictment on grounds of vagueness, the Court excluded any mention of the Thirteenth Amendment. It ignored Justice Bradley's lower court opinion, in which he reasoned that the Thirteenth Amendment provided constitutional authority for federal prosecution of racially motivated violence against African

Americans. The Court also failed to comment on Justice Bradley's distinction between ordinary crimes, which he saw as within the state's exclusive jurisdiction, and crimes of race, which he regarded as within the Thirteenth Amendment's guarantee of equality before the law.

While *Blyew* and *Cruikshank* eviserated the Amendment's grant of federal authority over race-related prosecutions, the *Slaughter-House Cases* [three cases consolidated for review of by Supreme Court], further constrained the application of the Thirteenth Amendment by narrowly defining involuntary servitude. In the *Slaughter-House Cases*, white butchers sought to invalidate a Louisiana law that granted monopoly rights to a slaughterhouse corporation and denied the butchers the use of their own land and property to pursue an occupation. They argued that it violated the Thirteenth Amendment's prohibition against involuntary servitude.

Narrowing the Thirteenth Amendment

Minimizing the Thirteenth Amendment's "grand yet simple declaration of the personal freedom of all the human race," the Court's 5–4 decision rejected the idea that granting a monopoly license to a corporation implicated liberty. The Court found that using "a microscopic search [to] endeavor to find [in the Thirteenth Amendment] a reference to servitudes, which may have been attached to property . . . requires an effort." The decision's sweeping language limited the Amendment's prohibition against involuntary servitude to the abolishment of chattel slavery.

Each of these three decisions evidenced the Court's narrowing of the Thirteenth Amendment. Several years after Reconstruction's formal ending, the Court further curtailed the power of the Thirteenth Amendment in the *Civil Rights Cases*. By declaring that Congress did not have the authority to eliminate slavery's badges and incidents, the Court rendered the Amendment moribund [nearly obsolete]. . . .

Laws Passed Following *Plessy v. Ferguson*		
Type	Number	Percentage of Total Statutes Passed
Miscengenation	127	29
Education	112	25
Public carrier	71	16
Public accommodation	34	8
Voting rights	29	6

TAKEN FROM: *The History of Jim Crow* Web site.

The *Civil Rights Cases* provided the conceptual framework for eviscerating the Thirteenth Amendment and for denying its use as a source of congressional power for protecting fundamental citizenship rights. Subsequent Court decisions in *Plessy v. Ferguson* and *Hodges v. United States* completely gutted the Amendment's substance and spirit, limiting its application to a dictionary definition of slavery.

The Impact of *Plessy v. Ferguson* and *Hodges v. United States*

In the *Civil Rights Cases*, the Supreme Court still unanimously agreed that the Thirteenth Amendment guaranteed universal civil and political freedom and the obliteration of slavery with all its badges and incidents. The majority specifically held that the Thirteenth Amendment nullified all state laws that establish or uphold slavery. Yet only a decade later, in *Plessy v. Ferguson*, eight Justices could "not understand" why the plaintiff relied upon that Amendment to challenge Louisiana's criminal law mandating the segregation of African Americans from white railway passengers.

The *Plessy* Court declared that mandated segregation did not violate the Thirteenth Amendment because it did not "stamp[] the colored race with a badge of inferiority." If African Americans felt otherwise, the majority proclaimed, it was "not by reason of anything found in the act, but solely because the colored race chooses to put that construction upon it." Appearing oblivious to congressional intent and to segregation's underpinning in slavery, the majority proclaimed that the drafters of the Thirteenth Amendment never intended that the abolition of slavery would require the prohibition of racially discriminatory state laws. The *Plessy* Court concluded that the Thirteenth Amendment only applied to the compulsory exploitation of labor and peonage.

Again Justice Harlan was the lone dissenting voice. He sought to revive the Thirteenth Amendment's purpose of eliminating all burdens and disadvantages that persisted as remnants of slavery or servitude. Because the Louisiana statute compelled African Americans to sit separately from white passengers, Harlan understood that it was intended to reinforce their racial inferiority. Justice Harlan found that the Amendment prohibited "the deprivation of any right necessarily inhering in freedom" and concluded that the arbitrary separation of citizens on the basis of race was wholly inconsistent with the Amendment's guarantee of freedom and equality before the law.

It would be more than seventy years before Justice Harlan's view was resurrected and accepted by a Supreme Court majority. His warning that *Plessy* would "in time, prove to be quite as pernicious as the decision made by this tribunal in the Dred Scott case" proved to be remarkably prescient. In the period immediately following *Plessy*, thousands of whites joined lynch mobs against African Americans and received virtual immunity from criminal prosecution.

The Court's 1906 decision in *Hodges v. United States* reinforced official tolerance of such lawlessness by overturning the federal conviction of several white defendants who had used violence and threats to force African American workers to surrender their jobs. The seven-Justice majority held that the Thirteenth Amendment did not authorize such criminal prosecutions.

Justice Brewer's majority opinion ignored the legislative history behind the Thirteenth Amendment and the 1866 Act and instead referred to Webster's dictionary. The Court adopted a plain language rule that prohibited only the compulsory service of one person to another. With this definition, the Court rejected its prior view as well as Reconstruction legislators' determination that federal legislation was necessary to eliminate slavery's badges and incidents.

The Court's interpretation was fueled by the general movement in favor of states' rights. The Brewer opinion scoffed at the Thirteenth Amendment's national protections and refused to consider whether the defendants' actions were intended to maintain white supremacy or to reinforce African Americans' racial inferiority and subjugation. Instead, the Court concluded that "no mere personal assault or trespass or appropriation operates to reduce the individual to a condition of slavery."

Writing in dissent, Justices Harlan and Day referred extensively to prior Thirteenth Amendment decisions in which the Court had found that the Amendment guaranteed universal freedom and abolished the perpetuation of slavery's badges and incidents. Both dissenting Justices considered the defendants' actions as falling squarely within the Amendment's prohibitions. They recognized that liberty rights are implicated whenever citizens are denied employment opportunities because of their race. They further observed that one of the incidents of slavery at the time of the adoption of the Thirteenth Amendment was the prohibition against slaves entering into contracts. Justices Harlan and Day found that the majority's holding paralyzed the federal government from prosecuting individuals who violently prevented citizens of color from earning a living. They concluded that their brethren's interpretation was hostile to the freedom established by the supreme law of the land, and that it neutralized many of the declarations made by the Thirteenth Amendment.

The Supreme Court's analysis in the *Civil Rights Cases, Plessy,* and *Hodges* limited the Amendment's application to situations involving compulsory labor or violations of anti-peonage laws. Consistent with the Court's restricted interpretation of the Thirteenth Amendment, legal scholars also paid scant attention to the Amendment's intended reach. For most of the Amendment's first century, scholars did not dispute the Supreme Court's doctrine and dogmatically advanced two themes: first, the Amendment's prohibitions applied only to situations involving enforced compulsory service; and second, the Amendment did not contain affirmative rights protections. In 1947, one commentator observed that "a refusal of the courts to give the Amendment its historical meaning has resulted in its retaining only a marginal importance today," adding that the "restricted definition is now so well-settled that this Amendment offers no basis for Congressional anti-racial discrimination legislation." Then, on the last day of the Warren Court, the Supreme Court decided *Jones v. Alfred H. Mayer Company* and resurrected the Amendment's nearly forgotten objectives.

Supreme Court Makes First Decision Regarding Amendments XIII and XIV

The New York Times

In its first decision regarding the Thirteenth and Fourteenth Amendments to the U.S. Constitution, the U.S. Supreme Court set an important precedent. The decision dealt with a case involving Louisiana butchers and slaughterhouses. Louisiana passed an act granting to a corporation created by the state the rights, buildings, and lands to open slaughterhouses. After the ratification of the Thirteenth and Fourteenth Amendments, butchers— white citizens—of New Orleans, Louisiana, brought suit against the Crescent City Live Stock Landing and Slaughter-house Company, employed by the state legislature of Louisiana. These butchers claimed that they were involved in involuntary servitude by having to work for state-regulated slaughterhouses and that their rights were being deprived by the state without the benefit of due process, a right that is explicitly granted to citizens by the Fourteenth Amendment under equal protection of the law. The Supreme Court, however, interpreted the Fourteenth Amendment through the authors' intentions of granting citizenship and equal protection of the law to freedmen. This editorial, which first appeared in The New York Times *on April 16, 1873, discusses the importance of the Supreme Court's opinion in the* Slaughter-House Cases. *The editorial voices the opinion that the Supreme Court ruled correctly in stating that the Thirteenth and Fourteenth Amendments were meant to grant citizenship to former slaves and to ensure that freedmen enjoyed equal protection of the law that would never be taken away without due process.*

The New York Times, "The Scope of the Thirteenth and Fourteenth Amendments," April 16, 1873, p. 6.

The Supreme Court has just rendered its first decision defining the scope of the Thirteenth and Fourteenth Amendments to the Federal Constitution. The opinion is very important, for several reasons. It is calculated to throw the immense moral force of the Court on the side of rational and careful interpretation of the rights of the States and those of the Union. It is calculated to maintain, and to add to, the respect felt for the Court, as being at once scrupulous in its regard for the Constitution, and unambitious of extending its own jurisdiction. It is also a severe and, we might almost hope, a fatal blow to that school of constitutional lawyers who have been engaged, ever since the adoption of the Fourteenth Amendment, in inventing impossible consequences for that addition to the Constitution.

Details of the Case

The decision referred to was in the case of certain New-Orleans butchers against the Crescent City Live Stock Landing and Slaughter-house Company. This company was incorporated three years ago by the Legislature of Louisiana. The act of incorporation gave it the exclusive privilege of erecting slaughter-houses and landings for live stock in the City of New-Orleans. On the other hand, the act required the company to provide buildings for slaughtering 500 animals each day, and to admit any person to slaughter animals in their slaughter-houses for certain fixed rates. The butchers claim that this act is contrary to the Thirteenth and Fourteenth Amendments of the United States Constitution, in that it creates an involuntary servitude, in that it abridges the privileges ... of citizens of the United States, in that it denies to the plaintiffs the equal protection of the laws, and in that it deprives them of their property without due process of law. The Supreme Court decides against the plaintiffs on all these points.

It holds, substantially, that the amendments must be construed by the light thrown by their history on the intention of the people in adopting them. The Court reviews this history, to show that the general purpose of the amendments was to protect the rights of the freedmen. To this end slavery was abolished by the Thirteenth Amendment. The servitude so done away with was personal servitude. It was of the kind that would include penal servitude, if that had not been distinctly excluded. It was not and could not be that subordination in matters of business and profit which it is not in the province of the National Constitution to regulate, and which the people did not intend to bring within the jurisdiction of the National Government. Similarly as to the provisions defining citizenship of the United States and of the several States, and securing the privileges and immunities of the former. By the record of the Supreme Court, the negro was denied the right of citizenship of the United States. He was recognized in some States and rejected in others as a citizen of the State in which he might happen to reside. The Fourteenth Amendment made him a citizen of the United States, and forbade any State to abridge his privileges and immunities as such. It also made him a citizen of the State in which he resides, and required that his rights of property and person shall be respected, and that he shall have equal protection of the laws. These provisions are, of course, general. But they were framed for the freedmen, and had not the condition of that great body of our people required it, the amendment never would have been passed. The Court holds, in substance, that this obvious fact in the history of the amendment must be considered in interpreting it; that the "privileges and immunities" it was intended to protect were the fundamental ones belonging to citizens of the United States as such, and not the specific ones, which vary in the several States; and that while it required each State to recognize the rights of the citizens of any other State as the same as those of its own citizens, it did not intend to deprive any State of the power of defining the rights of its own citizens. In short, the Fourteenth Amendment was not a piece of abstract declaration, meant to establish a general definition of rights for Congress to legislate for, and the Supreme Court to adjudicate on. It was a piece of practical legislation, meant to remove certain obvious evils, and to establish certain results which were the logical outgrowth of the war. The Court says:

"Was it the purpose of the framers of the Fourteenth Amendment, by the simple declaration that no State shall make or enforce any laws which shall abridge the privileges and immunities of citizens of the United States, to transfer the security and protection of all the civil rights which we have mentioned from the States to the Federal Government? And where it is declared that Congress shall have power to enforce that article, was it intended to bring within the power of Congress the entire domain of civil rights heretofore belonging exclusively to the States?

Future Impact of the Decision

All this and more must follow if this proposition of plaintiffs in error be sound; for not only are these rights subject to the control of Congress whenever, in its discretion, any of them are supposed to be abridged by State legislation, but that body may also pass laws in advance, limiting and resisting the exercise of legislative power by the States in their most ordinary and usual functions, as in its judgment or discretion it may think proper on all such subjects. And still further, such a construction, followed by the reversal of the judgments of the Supreme Court of Louisiana in these cases, would constitute this court a perpetual censor upon all legislation of the States on the civil rights of its own citizens, with authority to nullify such as it did not approve as consistent with those rights as they existed at the time of the adoption of this amendment. The argument, we admit, is not always the most conclusive where it draws from the consequences urged against the adoptions of a particular construction of an instrument. But when, as in the case before us, these consequences are so serious, so far-reaching and pervading, so great a departure from the structure and spirit of our institutions; when the effect is to falter and degrade the State Governments by subjecting them to the control of Congress in the exercise of powers heretofore universally conceded to them of the most ordinary and fundamental character; when, in fact, it radically changes the whole theory of the relations of the State and Federal Governments to each other, and of both these Governments to the people; the argument has force that is irresistible in the absence of language which expresses this purpose too clearly to need construction.

We are convinced that no such results were intended by the Congress which proposed these amendments, nor by the Legislatures of the States which ratified them.

Plessy v. Ferguson: "Separate but Equal" Segregation Laws Do Not Violate Amendment XIII

Henry Billings Brown

The U.S. Supreme Court set an unfortunate precedent with its Plessy v. Ferguson decision. This case involved an African American man named Homer Plessy, who attempted to fight segregation under the Thirteenth and Fourteenth Amendments. The majority opinion, written by Justice Henry Billings Brown, asserts that segregation is constitutional and does not violate either the Thirteenth or the Fourteenth Amendment. This decision established the "separate but equal" doctrine, which enabled states to continue Jim Crow laws well into the 1960s. The opinion, which states that segregation does not establish the white race as dominant, concludes that separate facilities do not deprive African American citizens of any privileges or rights. The decision also allows states to set laws defining what constitutes an African American citizen. Until it was overturned nearly sixty years later in Brown v. Board of Education of Topeka, Kansas *(1954),* Plessy *did limit the rights of African American citizens in the United States by legalizing segregation. Brown served on the Supreme Court from January 5, 1891, to May 28, 1906.*

That petitioner [Homer Plessy] was a citizen of the United States and a resident of the state of Louisiana, of mixed descent, in the proportion of seven-eighths Caucasian and one-eighth African blood; that the mixture of colored blood was not discernible in him, and that he was entitled to every recognition, right, privilege, and immunity secured to the citizens of the United States of the white race by its constitution and laws; that on June 7, 1892, he engaged and paid for a

Henry Billings Brown, Majority Opinion, *Plessy v. Ferguson*, 1896.

first-class passage on the East Louisiana Railway, from New Orleans to Covington, in the same state, and thereupon entered a passenger train, and took possession of a vacant seat in a coach where passengers of the white race were accommodated; that such railroad company was incorporated by the laws of Louisiana as a common carrier, and was not authorized to distinguish between citizens according to their race, but, notwithstanding this, petitioner was required by the conductor, under penalty of ejection from said train and imprisonment, to vacate said coach, and occupy another seat, in a coach assigned by said company for persons not of the white race, and for no other reason than that petitioner was of the colored race; that, upon petitioner's refusal to comply with such order, he was, with the aid of a police officer, forcibly ejected from said coach, and hurried off to, and imprisoned in, the parish jail of New Orleans, and there held to answer a charge made by such officer to the effect that he was guilty of having criminally violated an act of the general assembly of the state, approved July 10, 1890, in such case made and provided.

The petitioner was subsequently brought before the recorder of the city for preliminary examination, and committed for trial to the criminal district court for the parish of Orleans, where an information was filed against him in the matter above set forth, for a violation of the above act, which act the petitioner affirmed to be null and void, because in conflict with the constitution of the United States; that petitioner interposed a plea to such information, based upon the unconstitutionality of the act of the general assembly, to which the district attorney, on behalf of the state, filed a demurrer; that, upon issue being joined upon such demurrer and plea, the court sustained the demurrer, overruled the plea, and ordered petitioner to plead over to the facts set forth in the information, and that, unless the judge of the said court be enjoined by a writ of prohibition from further proceeding in such case, the court will proceed to fine and sentence petitioner to imprisonment, and thus deprive him of his constitutional rights set forth in his said plea, notwithstanding the unconstitutionality of the act under which he was being prosecuted; that no appeal lay from such sentence, and petitioner was without relief or remedy except by writs of prohibition and certiorari. . . .

The Start of Separate but Equal

The first section of the statute enacts 'that all railway companies carrying passengers in their coaches in this state, shall provide equal but separate accommodations for the white, and colored races, by providing two or more passenger coaches for each passenger train, or by dividing the passenger coaches by a partition so as to secure separate accommodations: provided, that this section shall not be construed to apply to street railroads. No person or persons shall be permitted to occupy seats in coaches, other than the ones assigned to them, on account of the race they belong to.'

By the second section it was enacted 'that the officers of such passenger trains shall have power and are hereby required to assign each passenger to the coach or compartment used for the race to which such passenger belongs; any passenger insisting on going into a coach or compartment to which by race he does not belong, shall be liable to a fine of twenty-five dollars, or in lieu thereof to imprisonment for a period of not more than twenty days in the parish prison, and any officer of any railroad insisting on assigning a passenger to a coach or compartment other than the one set aside for the race to which said passenger belongs, shall be liable to a fine of twenty-five dollars, or in lieu thereof to imprisonment for a period of not more than twenty days in the parish prison; and should any passenger refuse to occupy the coach or compartment to which he or she is assigned by the officer of such railway, said officer shall have power to refuse to carry such

Supreme Court justice Henry Billings Brown (1836–1913). The Library of Congress.

passenger on his train, and for such refusal neither he nor the railway company which he represents shall be liable for damages in any of the courts of this state.' . . .

The constitutionality of this act is attacked upon the ground that it conflicts both with the thirteenth amendment of the constitution, abolishing slavery, and the fourteenth amendment, which prohibits certain restrictive legislation on the part of the states.

That it does not conflict with the thirteenth amendment, which abolished slavery and involuntary servitude, except a punishment for crime, is too clear for argument. Slavery implies involuntary servitude,—a state of bondage; the ownership of mankind as a chattel, or, at least, the control of the labor and services of one man for the benefit of another, and the absence of a legal right to the disposal of his own person, property, and services. This amendment was said in the *Slaughter-House Cases* to have been intended primarily to abolish slavery, as it had been previously known in this country. . . . It was intimated, however, in that case, that this amendment was regarded by the statesmen of that day as insufficient to protect the colored race from certain laws which had been enacted in the Southern states, imposing upon the colored race onerous disabilities and burdens, and curtailing their rights in the pursuit of life, liberty, and property to such an extent that their freedom was of little value; and that the fourteenth amendment was devised to meet this exigency.

So, too, in the *Civil Rights Cases*, it was said that the act of a mere individual, the owner of an inn, a public conveyance or place of amusement, refusing accommodations to colored people, cannot be justly regarded as imposing any badge of slavery or servitude upon the applicant, but only as involving an ordinary civil injury, properly cognizable by the laws of the state, and presumably subject to redress by those laws until the contrary appears. . . .

A statute which implies merely a legal distinction between the white and colored races—a distinction which is founded in the color of the two races, and which must always exist so long as white men are distinguished from the other race by color—has no tendency to destroy the legal equality of the two races, or re-establish a state of involuntary servitude. Indeed, we do not understand that the thirteenth amendment is strenuously relied upon by the plaintiff in error in this connection.

By the fourteenth amendment, all persons born or naturalized in the United States, and subject to the jurisdiction thereof, are made citizens of the United States and of the state wherein they reside; and the states are forbidden from making or enforcing any law which shall abridge the privileges or immunities of citizens of the United States, or shall deprive any person of life, liberty, or property without due process of law, or deny to any person within their jurisdiction the equal protection of the laws.

The proper construction of this amendment was first called to the attention of this court in the *Slaughter-House Cases*, which involved, however, not a question of race, but one of exclusive privileges. The case did not call for any expression of opinion as to the exact rights it was intended to secure to the colored race, but it was said generally that its main purpose was to establish the citizenship of the negro, to give definitions of citizenship of the United States and of the states, and to protect from the hostile legislation of the states the privileges and immunities of citizens of the United States, as distinguished from those of citizens of the states. The object of the amendment was undoubtedly to enforce the absolute equality of the two races before the law, but, in the nature of things, it could not have been intended to abolish distinctions based upon color, or to enforce social, as distinguished from political, equality, or a commingling of the two races upon terms unsatisfactory to either. Laws permitting, and even requiring, their separation, in places where they are liable to be brought into contact, do not necessarily imply the inferiority of either race to the other, and have been generally, if not universally, recognized as within the competency of the state legislatures in the exercise of their police power. . . .

The distinction between laws interfering with the political equality of the negro and those requiring the separation of the two races in schools, theaters, and railway carriages has been frequently drawn by this court. . . . So, where the laws of a particular locality or the charter of a particular railway corporation has provided that no person shall be excluded from the cars on account of color, we have held that this meant that persons of color should travel in the same car as white ones, and that the enactment was not satisfied by the company providing cars assigned exclusively to people of color, though they were as good as those which they assigned exclusively to white persons. . . .

In the *Civil Rights Cases*, it was held that an act of congress entitling all persons within the jurisdiction of the United States to the full and equal enjoyment of the accommodations, advantages, facilities, and privileges of inns, public conveyances, on land or water, theaters, and other places of public amusement, and made applicable to citizens of every race and color, regardless of any previous condition of servitude, was unconstitutional and void, upon the ground that the fourteenth amendment was prohibitory upon the states only, and the legislation authorized to be adopted by congress for enforcing it was not direct legislation on matters respecting which the states were prohibited from making or enforcing certain laws, or doing certain acts, but was corrective legislation, such as might be necessary or proper for counter-acting and redressing the effect of such laws or acts. In delivering the opinion of the court, Mr. Justice [Joseph P.] Bradley observed that the fourteenth amendment 'does not invest congress with power to legislate upon subjects that are within the domain of state legislation, but to provide modes of relief against state legislation or state action of the kind referred to. It does not authorize congress to create a code of municipal law for the regulation of private rights, but to provide modes of redress against the operation of state laws, and the action of state officers, executive or judicial, when these are subversive of the fundamental rights specified in the amendment. Positive rights and privileges are undoubtedly secured by the fourteenth amendment; but they are secured by way of prohibition against state laws and state proceedings affecting those rights and privileges, and by power given to congress to legislate for the purpose of carrying such prohibition into effect; and such legislation must necessarily be predicated upon such supposed state laws or state proceedings, and be directed to the correction of their operation and effect.'

Much nearer, and, indeed, almost directly in point, is the case of the Louisville, *N. O. & T. Ry. Co. v. State*, wherein the railway company was indicted for a violation of a statute of Mississippi, enacting that all railroads carrying passengers should provide equal, but separate, accommodations for the white and colored races, by providing two or more passenger cars for each passenger train, or by dividing the passenger cars by a partition, so as to secure separate accommodations. The case was presented in a different aspect from the one under consideration, inasmuch as it was an indictment against the railway company for failing to provide the separate accommodations, but the question considered was the constitutionality of the law. In that case, the supreme court of Mississippi had held that the statute applied solely to commerce within the state, and, that being the construction of the state statute by its highest court, was accepted as conclusive. 'If it be a matter,' said the court, 'respecting commerce wholly within a state, and not interfering with commerce between the states, then, obviously, there is no violation of the commerce clause of the federal constitution. . . . No question arises under this section as to the power of the state to separate in different compartments interstate passengers, or affect, in any manner, the privileges and rights of such passengers. All that we can consider is whether the state has the power to require that railroad trains within her limits shall have separate accommodations for the two races. That affecting only commerce within the state is no invasion of the power given to congress by the commerce clause.'

A like course of reasoning applies to the case under consideration, since the supreme court of Louisiana, in the case of *State v. Judge*, held that the statute in question did not apply to interstate passengers, but was confined in its application to passengers traveling exclusively within the borders of the state. The case was decided largely upon the authority of Louisville, *N. O. & T. Ry. Co. v. State* and affirmed by this court. In the present case no question of interference with interstate commerce can possibly arise, since the East Louisiana Railway appears to have been purely a local line, with both its termini within the state of Louisiana. Similar statutes for the separation of the two races upon public conveyances were held to be constitutional. . . .

The Court's Decision

While we think the enforced separation of the races, as applied to the internal commerce of the state, neither abridges the privileges or immunities of the colored man, deprives him of his property without due process of law, nor denies him the equal protection of the laws, within the meaning of the fourteenth amendment, we are not prepared to say that the conductor, in assigning passengers to the coaches according to their race, does not act at his peril, or that the provision of the second section of the act that denies to the passenger compensation in damages for a refusal to receive him into the coach in which he properly belongs is a valid exercise of the legislative power. Indeed, we understand it to be conceded by the state's attorney that such part of the act as exempts from liability the railway company and its officers is unconstitutional. The power to assign to a particular coach obviously implies the power to determine to which race the passenger belongs, as well as the power to determine who, under the laws of the particular state, is to be deemed a white, and who a colored, person. . . .

In this connection, it is also suggested by the learned counsel for the plaintiff in error that the same argument that will justify the state legislature in requiring railways to provide separate accommodations for the two races will also authorize them to require separate cars to be provided for people whose hair is of a certain color, or who are aliens, or who belong to certain nationalities, or to enact laws requiring colored people to walk upon one side of the street, and white people upon the other, or requiring white men's houses to be painted white, and colored men's black, or their vehicles or business signs to be of different colors, upon the theory that one side of the street is as good as the other, or that a house or vehicle of one color is as good as one of another color. The reply to all this is that every exercise of the police power must be reasonable, and extend only to such laws as are enacted in good faith for the promotion of the public good, and not for the annoyance or oppression of a particular class. . . .

So far, then, as a conflict with the fourteenth amendment is concerned, the case reduces itself to the question whether the statute of Louisiana is a reasonable regulation, and with respect to this there must necessarily be a large discretion on the part of the legislature. In determining the question of reasonableness, it is at liberty to act with reference to the established usages, customs, and traditions of the people, and with a view to the promotion of their comfort, and the preservation of the public peace and good order. Gauged by this standard, we cannot say that a law which authorizes or even requires the separation of the two races in public conveyances is unreasonable, or more obnoxious to the fourteenth amendment than the acts of congress requiring separate schools for colored children in the District of Columbia, the constitutionality of which does not seem to have been questioned, or the corresponding acts of state legislatures.

We consider the underlying fallacy of the plaintiff's argument to consist in the assumption that the enforced separation of the two races stamps the colored race with a badge of inferiority. If this be so, it is not by reason of anything found in the act, but solely because the colored race chooses to put that construction upon it. The argument necessarily assumes that if, as has been more than once the case, and is not unlikely to be so again, the colored race should become the dominant power in the state legislature, and should enact a law in precisely similar terms, it would thereby relegate the white race to an inferior position. We imagine that the white race, at least, would not acquiesce in this assumption. The argument also assumes that social prejudices may be overcome by legislation, and that equal rights cannot be secured to the negro except by an enforced commingling of the two races. We cannot accept this proposition. If the two races are to meet upon terms of social equality, it must be the result of natural affinities, a mutual appreciation of each other's merits and a voluntary consent of individuals. . . . Legislation is powerless to eradicate racial instincts, or to abolish distinctions based upon physical differences, and the attempt to do so can only result in accentuating the difficulties of the present situation. If the civil and political rights of both races be equal, one cannot be inferior to the other civilly or politically. If one race be inferior to the other socially, the constitution of the United States cannot put them upon the same plane.

It is true that the question of the proportion of colored blood necessary to constitute a colored person, as distinguished from a white person, is one upon which there is a difference of opinion in the different states. . . . But these are questions to be determined under the laws of each state, and are not properly put in issue in this case. Under the allegations of his petition, it may undoubtedly become a question of importance whether, under the laws of Louisiana, the petitioner belongs to the white or colored race.

Jones v. Mayer Co.: Housing Developer Pins "Badge of Slavery" on African American Buyer

Potter Stewart

Decided in the midst of the civil rights movement, Jones v. Mayer Co. (1968) first states that 42 U.S.C. § 1982, an Act of Congress, is constitutional. The decision, written by Potter Stewart, also asserts that the act allows Congress to regulate the sale of private property effectively to prevent racial discrimination and that it bars all racial discrimination in the sale of property. In just this one case, the Warren Court, known for the liberalism of Chief Justice Earl Warren and many of its associate justices, overturned many of the decisions made by Supreme Courts before it. Stewart served on the Supreme Court from October 14, 1958, to July 3, 1981.

In this case we are called upon to determine the scope and the constitutionality of an Act of Congress, 42 U.S.C. 1982, which provides that:

> "All citizens of the United States shall have the same right, in every State and Territory, as is enjoyed by white citizens thereof to inherit, purchase, lease, sell, hold, and convey real and personal property."

On September 2, 1965, the petitioners [Joseph Lee Jones] filed a complaint in the District Court for the Eastern District of Missouri, alleging that the respondents [Alfred H. Mayer Co.] had refused to sell them a home in the Paddock Woods community of St. Louis County for the sole reason that petitioner Joseph Lee Jones is a Negro. Relying in part upon 1982, the petitioners sought injunctive and other relief. The District

Potter Stewart, Majority Opinion, *Jones v. Mayer Co.*, 1968.

Court sustained the respondents' motion to dismiss the complaint, and the Court of Appeals for the Eighth Circuit affirmed, concluding that 1982 applies only to state action and does not reach private refusals to sell. We granted certiorari to consider the questions thus presented. For the reasons that follow, we reverse the judgment of the Court of Appeals. We hold that 1982 bars all racial discrimination, private as well as public, in the sale or rental of property, and that the statute, thus construed, is a valid exercise of the power of Congress to enforce the Thirteenth Amendment.

At the outset, it is important to make clear precisely what this case does not involve. Whatever else it may be, 42 U.S.C. 1982 is not a comprehensive open housing law. In sharp contrast to the Fair Housing Title (Title VIII) of the Civil Rights Act of 1968, the statute in this case deals only with racial discrimination and does not address itself to discrimination on grounds of religion or national origin. It does not deal specifically with discrimination in the provision of services or facilities in connection with the sale or rental of a dwelling. It does not prohibit advertising or other representations that indicate discriminatory preferences. It does not refer explicitly to discrimination in financing arrangements or in the provision of brokerage services. It does not empower a federal administrative agency to assist aggrieved parties. It makes no provision for intervention by the Attorney General. And, although it can be enforced by injunction, it contains no provision expressly authorizing a federal court to order the payment of damages.

Thus, although 1982 contains none of the exemptions that Congress included in the Civil Rights Act of 1968, it would be a serious mistake to suppose that 1982 in any way diminishes the significance of the law recently enacted by Congress. Indeed, the Senate Subcommittee on Housing and Urban Affairs was informed in hearings held after the Court of Appeals had rendered its decision in this case that 1982 might well be "a presently valid federal statutory ban against discrimination by private persons in the sale or lease of real property." The Sub-committee was told, however, that even if this Court should so construe 1982, the existence of that statute would not "eliminate the need for congressional action" to spell out "responsibility on the part of the federal government to enforce the rights it protects." The point was made that, in light of the many difficulties confronted by private litigants seeking to enforce such rights on their own, "legislation is needed to establish federal machinery for enforcement of the rights guaranteed under Section 1982 of Title 42 even if the plaintiffs in *Jones v. Alfred H. Mayer Company* should prevail in the United States Supreme Court. . . ."

This Court last had occasion to consider the scope of 42 U.S.C. 1982 in 1948, in *Hurd v. Hodge.* That case arose when property owners in the District of Columbia sought to enforce racially restrictive covenants against the Negro purchasers of several homes on their block. A federal district court enforced the restrictive agreements by declaring void the deeds of the Negro purchasers. It enjoined further attempts to sell or lease them the properties in question and directed them to "remove themselves and all of their personal belongings" from the premises within 60 days. The Court of Appeals for the District of Columbia Circuit affirmed, and this Court granted certiorari to decide whether 1982, then 1978 of the Revised Statutes of 1874, barred enforcement of the racially restrictive agreements in that case.

The agreements in *Hurd* covered only two-thirds of the lots of a single city block, and preventing Negroes from buying or renting homes in that specific area would not have rendered them ineligible to do so elsewhere in the city. Thus, if 1982 had been thought to do no more than grant Negro citizens the legal capacity to buy and rent property free of prohibitions that wholly disabled them because of their race, judicial enforcement of the restrictive covenants at issue would not have violated 1982. But this Court took a broader view of the statute. Although the covenants could have been enforced without denying the general right of Negroes to purchase or lease real estate, the enforcement of those covenants would nonetheless have denied the Negro purchasers "the same right 'as is enjoyed by white citizens . . . to inherit, purchase, lease, sell, hold, and convey real and personal property.'" That result, this Court concluded, was prohibited by 1982. To suggest otherwise, the Court said, "is to reject the plain meaning of language." . . .

Examining Statute 1982

We begin with the language of the statute itself. In plain and unambiguous terms, 1982 grants to all citizens, without regard to race or color, "the same right" to purchase and lease property "as is enjoyed by white citizens." As the Court of Appeals in this case evidently recognized, that right can be impaired as effectively by "those who place property on the market" as by the State itself. For, even if the State and its agents lend no support to those who wish to exclude persons from their communities on racial grounds, the fact remains that, whenever property "is placed on the market for whites only, whites have a right denied to Negroes." So long as a Negro citizen who wants to buy or rent a home can be turned away simply because he is not white, he cannot be said to enjoy "the same right . . . as is enjoyed by white citizens . . . to . . . purchase [and] lease . . . real and personal property."

On its face, therefore, 1982 appears to prohibit all discrimination against Negroes in the sale or rental of property—discrimination by private owners as well as discrimination by public authorities. Indeed, even the respondents seem to concede that, if 1982 "means what it says"—to use the words of the respondents' brief—then it must encompass every racially motivated refusal to sell or rent and cannot be confined to officially sanctioned segregation in housing. Stressing what they consider to be the revolutionary implications of so literal a reading of 1982, the respondents argue that Congress cannot possibly have intended any such result. Our examination of the relevant history, however, persuades us that Congress meant exactly what it said. . . .

The crucial language for our purposes was that which guaranteed all citizens "the same right, in every State and Territory in the United States, . . . to inherit, purchase, lease, sell, hold, and convey real and personal property . . . as is enjoyed by white citizens. . . ." To the Congress that passed the Civil Rights Act of 1866, it was clear that the right to do these things might be infringed not only by "State or local law" but also by "custom, or prejudice." Thus, when Congress provided in 1 of the Civil Rights Act that the right to purchase and lease property was to be enjoyed equally throughout the United States by Negro and white citizens alike, it plainly meant to secure that right against interference from any source whatever, whether governmental or private.

Indeed, if 1 had been intended to grant nothing more than an immunity from governmental interference, then much of 2 would have made no sense at all. For that section, which provided fines and prison terms for certain individuals who deprived others of rights "secured or protected" by 1, was carefully drafted to exempt private violations of 1 from the criminal sanctions it imposed. There would, of course, have been no private violations to exempt if the only "right" granted by 1 had been a right to be free of discrimination by public officials. Hence the structure of the 1866 Act, as well as its language, points to the conclusion urged by the petitioners in this case—that 1 was meant to prohibit all racially motivated deprivations of the rights enumerated in the statute, although only those deprivations perpetrated "under color of law" were to be criminally punishable under 2.

In attempting to demonstrate the contrary, the respondents rely heavily upon the fact that the Congress which ap-

proved the 1866 statute wished to eradicate the recently enacted Black Code—laws which had saddled Negroes with
"onerous disabilities and burdens, and curtailed their rights
... to such an extent that their freedom was of little value. ..."
[quoting the *Slaughter-House Cases* decision of 1873]. The respondents suggest that the only evil Congress sought to eliminate was that of racially discriminatory laws in the former
Confederate States. But the Civil Rights Act was drafted to apply throughout the country, and its language was far broader
than would have been necessary to strike down discriminatory
statutes.

That broad language, we are asked to believe, was a mere
slip of the legislative pen. We disagree. For the same Congress
that wanted to do away with the Black Codes also had before
it an imposing body of evidence pointing to the mistreatment
of Negroes by private individuals and unofficial groups, mistreatment unrelated to any hostile state legislation. "Accounts
in newspapers North and South, Freedmen's Bureau and other
official documents, private reports and correspondence were
all adduced" to show that "private outrage and atrocity" were
"daily inflicted on freedmen. ..." The congressional debates
are replete with references to private injustices against Negroes—references to white employers who refused to pay their
Negro workers, white planters who agreed among themselves
not to hire freed slaves without the permission of their former
masters, white citizens who assaulted Negroes or who combined to drive them out of their communities.

Indeed, one of the most comprehensive studies then before Congress stressed the prevalence of private hostility toward Negroes and the need to protect them from the resulting
persecution and discrimination. The report noted the existence of laws virtually prohibiting Negroes from owning or
renting property in certain towns, but described such laws as
"mere isolated cases," representing "the local outcroppings of a
spirit ... found to prevail everywhere"—a spirit expressed, for

example, by lawless acts of brutality directed against Negroes who traveled to areas where they were not wanted. The report concluded that, even if anti-Negro legislation were "repealed in all the States lately in rebellion," equal treatment for the Negro would not yet be secured.

In this setting, it would have been strange indeed if Congress had viewed its task as encompassing merely the nullification of racist laws in the former rebel States. That the Congress which assembled in the Nation's capital in December 1865 in fact had a broader vision of the task before it became clear early in the session, when three proposals to invalidate discriminatory state statutes were rejected as "too narrowly conceived." From the outset it seemed clear, at least to Senator [Lyman] Trumbull of Illinois, Chairman of the Judiciary Committee, that stronger legislation might prove necessary. . . .

Of course, Senator Trumbull's bill would, as he pointed out, "destroy all [the] discriminations" embodied in the Black Codes, but it would do more: It would affirmatively secure for all men, whatever their race or color, what the Senator called the "great fundamental rights":

> "the right to acquire property, the right to go and come at pleasure, the right to enforce rights in the courts, to make contracts, and to inherit and dispose of property."

As to those basic civil rights, the Senator said, the bill would "break down all discrimination between black men and white men." . . .

In the House, as in the Senate, much was said about eliminating the infamous Black Codes. But, like the Senate, the House was moved by a larger objective—that of giving real content to the freedom guaranteed by the Thirteenth Amendment. . . .

It thus appears that, when the House passed the Civil Rights Act on March 13, 1866, it did so on the same assumption that had prevailed in the Senate: It too believed that it was approving a comprehensive statute forbidding all racial discrimination affecting the basic civil rights enumerated in the Act. . . .

Against this background, it would obviously make no sense to assume, without any historical support whatever, that Congress made a silent decision in 1870 to exempt private discrimination from the operation of the Civil Rights Act of 1866. . . .

As we said in a somewhat different setting two Terms ago [in *United States v. Price*], "We think that history leaves no doubt that, if we are to give [the law] the scope that its origins dictate, we must accord it a sweep as broad as its language. . . . We are not at liberty to seek ingenious analytical instruments," to carve from 1982 an exception for private conduct—even though its application to such conduct in the present context is without established precedent. And, as the Attorney General of the United States said at the oral argument of this case, "The fact that the statute lay partially dormant for many years cannot be held to diminish its force today."

What Power Does Congress Have?

The remaining question is whether Congress has power under the Constitution to do what 1982 purports to do: to prohibit all racial discrimination, private and public, in the sale and rental of property. Our starting point is the Thirteenth Amendment, for it was pursuant to that constitutional provision that Congress originally enacted what is now 1982. . . .

Thus, the fact that 1982 operates upon the unofficial acts of private individuals, whether or not sanctioned by state law, presents no constitutional problem. If Congress has power under the Thirteenth Amendment to eradicate conditions that prevent Negroes from buying and renting property because of their race or color, then no federal statute calculated to achieve that objective can be thought to exceed the constitutional power of Congress simply because it reaches beyond state action to regulate the conduct of private individuals. The constitutional question in this case, therefore, comes to this: Does the authority of Congress to enforce the Thirteenth Amendment "by appropriate legislation" include the power to eliminate all racial barriers to the acquisition of real and personal property? We think the answer to that question is plainly yes. . . .

The True Scope of the Thirteenth Amendment

Those who opposed passage of the Civil Rights Act of 1866 argued in effect that the Thirteenth Amendment merely authorized Congress to dissolve the legal bond by which the Negro slave was held to his master. Yet many had earlier opposed the Thirteenth Amendment on the very ground that it would give Congress virtually unlimited power to enact laws for the protection of Negroes in every State. And the majority leaders in Congress—who were, after all, the authors of the Thirteenth Amendment—had no doubt that its Enabling Clause contemplated the sort of positive legislation that was embodied in the 1866 Civil Rights Act. . . .

Surely Congress has the power under the Thirteenth Amendment rationally to determine what are the badges and the incidents of slavery, and the authority to translate that determination into effective legislation. Nor can we say that the determination Congress has made is an irrational one. For this Court recognized long ago [in *Civil Rights Cases*] that, whatever else they may have encompassed, the badges and incidents of slavery—its "burdens and disabilities"—included restraints upon "those fundamental rights which are the essence of civil freedom, namely, the same right . . . to inherit, purchase, lease, sell and convey property, as is enjoyed by white citizens." Just as the Black Codes, enacted after the Civil War to restrict the free exercise of those rights, were substitutes for the slave system, so the exclusion of Negroes from white communities became a substitute for the Black Codes. And when racial discrimination herds men into ghettos and makes their ability to buy property turn on the color of their skin, then it too is a relic of slavery.

Negro citizens, North and South, who saw in the Thirteenth Amendment a promise of freedom—freedom to "go and come at pleasure" and to "buy and sell when they please"—would be left with "a mere paper guarantee" if Congress were powerless to assure that a dollar in the hands of a Negro will purchase the same thing as a dollar in the hands of a white man. At the very least, the freedom that Congress is empowered to secure under the Thirteenth Amendment includes the freedom to buy whatever a white man can buy, the right to live wherever a white man can live. If Congress cannot say that being a free man means at least this much, then the Thirteenth Amendment made a promise the Nation cannot keep.

Jones v. Mayer Co.: Majority Decision Interferes with Individual Rights

John Marshall Harlan II

John Marshall Harlan II, grandson of the lone dissenter of Plessy v. Ferguson, *wrote the dissenting opinion in* Jones v. Mayer Co. *His dissenting opinion states that the Court used the Thirteenth Amendment to defend a loosely worded statute (42 U.S.C. § 1982) and that "the Court's construction of 1982 as applying to purely private action is almost surely wrong, and at the least is open to serious doubt." Harlan did not write this dissenting opinion to deprive African American citizens of their rights, nor did he write this opinion to condone racial prejudice and discrimination. Harlan believed that the* Jones v. Mayer Co. *majority opinion, which allowed Congress to regulate the sale of private property, interfered with individual rights more than should be allowed. Harlan served on the Supreme Court from March 28, 1955, to September 23, 1971.*

The decision in this case appears to me to be most ill-considered and ill-advised.

The petitioners [Joseph Lee Jones] argue that the respondents' [Alfred M. Mayer Co.] racially motivated refusal to sell them a house entitles them to judicial relief on two separate grounds. First, they claim that the respondents acted in violation of 42 U.S.C. 1982; second, they assert that the respondents' conduct amounted in the circumstances to "state action" and was therefore forbidden by the Fourteenth Amendment even in the absence of any statute. The Court, without reaching the second ground alleged, holds that the petitioners

John Marshall Harlan II, Dissenting Opinion, *Jones v. Mayer Co.*, 1968.

are entitled to relief under 42 U.S.C. 1982, and that 1982 is constitutional as legislation appropriate to enforce the Thirteenth Amendment.

For reasons which follow, I believe that the Court's construction of 1982 as applying to purely private action is almost surely wrong, and at the least is open to serious doubt. The issues of the constitutionality of 1982, as construed by the Court, and of liability under the Fourteenth Amendment alone, also present formidable difficulties. Moreover, the political processes of our own era have, since the date of oral argument in this case, given birth to a civil rights statute embodying "fair housing" provisions which would at the end of this year make available to others, though apparently not to the petitioners themselves, the type of relief which the petitioners now seek. It seems to me that this latter factor so diminishes the public importance of this case that by far the wisest course would be for this Court to refrain from decision and to dismiss the writ as improvidently granted. . . .

The Court's opinion focuses upon the statute's legislative history, but it is worthy of note that the precedents in this Court are distinctly opposed to the Court's view of the statute. . . .

Like the Court, I begin analysis of 1982 by examining its language. In its present form, the section provides:

> "All citizens of the United States shall have the same right, in every State and Territory, as is enjoyed by white citizens thereof to inherit, purchase, lease, sell, hold, and convey real and personal property."

The Court finds it "plain and unambiguous," that this language forbids purely private as well as state-authorized discrimination. With all respect, I do not find it so. For me, there is an inherent ambiguity in the term "right," as used in 1982. The "right" referred to may either be a right to equal status under the law, in which case the statute operates only against state-sanctioned discrimination, or it may be an "absolute" right enforceable against private individuals. To me, the words of the statute, taken alone, suggest the former interpretation, not the latter....

Examining the Language

It seems to me that this original wording indicates even more strongly than the present language that 1 of the Act (as well as 2, which is explicitly so limited) was intended to apply only to action taken pursuant to state or community authority, in the form of a "law, statute, ordinance, regulation, or custom." And with deference I suggest that the language of 2, taken alone, no more implies that 2 "was carefully drafted to exempt private violations of 1 from the criminal sanctions it imposed," see ante, at 425, than it does that 2 was carefully drafted to enforce all of the rights secured by 1....

The First Session of the Thirty-ninth Congress met on December 4, 1865, some six months after the preceding Congress had sent to the States the Thirteenth Amendment, and a few days before word was received of that Amendment's ratification. On December 13, Senator [Charles] Wilson introduced a bill which would have invalidated all laws in the former rebel States which discriminated among persons as to civil rights on the basis of color, and which would have made it a misdemeanor to enact or enforce such a statute....

Senator Lyman Trumbull then indicated that he would introduce separate bills to enlarge the powers of the recently founded Freedmen's Bureau and to secure the freedmen in their civil rights, both bills in his view being authorized by the second clause of the Thirteenth Amendment. Since he had just stated that the purpose of that clause was to enable Congress to nullify acts of the state legislatures, it seems inferable that this was also to be the aim of the promised bills.

On January 5 [1866] Senator Trumbull introduced both the Freedmen's bill and the civil rights bill. The Freedmen's bill would have strengthened greatly the existing system by which agents of the Freedmen's Bureau exercised protective supervision over freedmen wherever they were present in large numbers. . . .

The form of the Freedmen's bill also undercuts the Court's argument that if 1 of the Civil Rights Act were construed as extending only to "state action," then "much of 2 [which clearly was so limited] would have made no sense at all." For the similar structure of the companion Freedmen's bill, drafted by the same hand and largely parallel in structure, would seem to confirm that the limitation to "state action" was deliberate.

The civil rights bill was debated intermittently in the Senate from January 12, 1866, until its eventual passage over the President's veto on April 6. In the course of the debates, Senator Trumbull, who was by far the leading spokesman for the bill, made a number of statements which can only be taken to mean that the bill was aimed at "state action" alone. For example, on January 29, 1866, Senator Trumbull began by citing a number of recently enacted Southern laws depriving men of rights named in the bill. He stated that "[t]he purpose of the bill under consideration is to destroy all these discriminations, and carry into effect the constitutional amendment." . . .

The remarks . . . constitute the plainest possible statement that the civil rights bill was intended to apply only to state-sanctioned conduct and not to purely private action. The Court has attempted to negate the force of these statements by citing other declarations by Senator Trumbull and others that the bill would operate everywhere in the country. However, the obvious and natural way to reconcile these two sets of statements is to read the ones about the bill's nationwide application as declarations that the enactment of a racially discriminatory law in any State would bring the bill into effect there. It seems to me that very great weight must be given these statements of Senator Trumbull, for they were clearly made to reassure Northern and Border State Senators about the extent of the bill's operation in their States. . . .

If the bill had been intended to reach purely private discrimination it seems very strange that Senator Trumbull did not think it necessary to defend the surely more dubious federal jurisdiction over cases involving no state action whatsoever. On April 4, Senator Trumbull reiterated that his reason for introducing the civil rights bill was to bring about "the passage of a law by Congress, securing equality in civil rights when denied by State authorities to freedmen and all other inhabitants of the United States. . . ."

The Intent of Congress

The Court puts forward in support of its construction an impressive number of quotations from and citations to the Senate debates. However, upon more circumspect analysis than the Court has chosen to give, virtually all of these appear to be either irrelevant or equally consistent with a "state action" interpretation. The Court's mention of a reference in the Senate debates to "white employers who refused to pay their Negro workers" surely does not militate against a "state action" construction, since "state action" would include conduct pursuant to "custom," and there was a very strong "custom" of refusing to pay slaves for work done. The Court's citation of Senate references to "white citizens who assaulted Negroes" is not in point, for the debate cited by the Court concerned the Freedmen's bill, not the civil rights bill. The former by its terms forbade discrimination pursuant to "prejudice," as well as "custom," and in any event neither bill provided a remedy for the victim of a racially motivated assault. . . .

The Court quotes and cites a number of passages from the House debates in aid of its construction of the bill. As in the case of the Senate debates, most of these appear upon close examination to provide little support. The first significant citation is a dialogue between Representative Wilson and Representative Loan, another of the bill's supporters. . . .

The interpretation which the Court places on Representative Wilson's remarks is a conceivable one. However, it is equally likely that, since both participants in the dialogue professed concern solely with 2 of the bill, their remarks carried no implication about the scope of 1. Moreover, it is possible to read the entire exchange as concerned with discrimination in communities having discriminatory laws, with Representative Loan urging that the laws should be abrogated directly or that all persons, not merely officers, who discriminated pursuant to them should be criminally punishable.

The next significant reliance upon the House debates is the Court's mention of references in the debates "to white employers who refused to pay their Negro workers, white planters who agreed among themselves not to hire freed slaves without the permission of their former masters, white citizens who assaulted Negroes or who combined to drive them out of their communities." As was pointed out in the discussion of the Senate debates, the references to white men's refusals to pay freedmen and their agreements not to hire freedmen without their "masters'" consent are by no means contrary to a "state action" view of the civil rights bill, since the bill expressly forbade action pursuant to "custom" and both of these practices reflected "customs" from the time of slavery. The Court cites two different House references to assaults on Negroes by whites. The first was by Congressman Windom, and close examination reveals that his only mention of assaults was with regard to a Texas "pass system," under which freedmen were whipped if found abroad without passes, and a South Carolina law permitting freedmen to be whipped for insolence. Since these assaults were sanctioned by law, or at least by "custom," they would be reached by the bill even under a "state action" interpretation. The other allusion to assaults, as well as the mention of combinations of whites to drive freedmen from communities, occurred in a speech by Representative Lawrence. . . .

The Court quotes a statement of Representative Eldridge, an opponent of the bill, in which he mentioned references by the bill's supporters to "individual cases of wrong perpetrated upon 'the freedmen of the South. . . .'" However, up to that time there had been no mention whatever in the House debates of any purely private discrimination, so one can only conclude that by "individual cases" Representative Eldridge meant "isolated cases," not "cases of purely private discrimination."

The last significant reference by the Court to the House debates is its statement that "Representative Cook of Illinois thought that, without appropriate federal legislation, any combination of men in [a] neighborhood [could] prevent [a Negro] from having any chance' to enjoy" the benefits of the Thirteenth Amendment. This quotation seems to be taken out of context. . . .

Concerns over Congress's Power

The foregoing analysis of the language, structure, and legislative history of the 1866 Civil Rights Act shows, I believe, that the Court's thesis that the Act was meant to extend to purely private action is open to the most serious doubt, if indeed it does not render that thesis wholly untenable. Another, albeit less tangible, consideration points in the same direction. Many of the legislators who took part in the congressional debates inevitably must have shared the individualistic ethic of their time, which emphasized personal freedom and embodied a distaste for governmental interference which was soon to culminate in the era of laissez-faire. It seems to me that most of these men would have regarded it as a great intrusion on individual liberty for the Government to take from a man the power to refuse for personal reasons to enter into a purely private transaction involving the disposition of property, albeit those personal reasons might reflect racial bias. It should be remembered that racial prejudice was not uncommon in

1866, even outside the South. . . . There were no state "fair housing" laws in 1866, and it appears that none had ever been proposed. In this historical context, I cannot conceive that a bill thought to prohibit purely private discrimination not only in the sale or rental of housing but in all property transactions would not have received a great deal of criticism explicitly directed to this feature. The fact that the 1866 Act received no criticism of this kind is for me strong additional evidence that it was not regarded as extending so far.

In sum, the most which can be said with assurance about the intended impact of the 1866 Civil Rights Act upon purely private discrimination is that the Act probably was envisioned by most members of Congress as prohibiting official, community-sanctioned discrimination in the South, engaged in pursuant to local "customs" which in the recent time of slavery probably were embodied in laws or regulations. Acts done under the color of such "customs" were, of course, said by the Court in the Civil Rights Cases, to constitute "state action" prohibited by the Fourteenth Amendment. Adoption of a "state action" construction of the Civil Rights Act would therefore have the additional merit of bringing its interpretation into line with that of the Fourteenth Amendment, which this Court has consistently held to reach only "state action." This seems especially desirable in light of the wide agreement that a major purpose of the Fourteenth Amendment, at least in the minds of its congressional proponents, was to assure that the rights conferred by the then recently enacted Civil Rights Act could not be taken away by a subsequent Congress.

The foregoing, I think, amply demonstrates that the Court has chosen to resolve this case by according to a loosely worded statute a meaning which is open to the strongest challenge in light of the statute's legislative history. In holding that the Thirteenth Amendment is sufficient constitutional authority for 1982 as interpreted, the Court also decides a question of great importance. Even contemporary supporters of the aims of the 1866 Civil Rights Act doubted that those goals could constitutionally be achieved under the Thirteenth Amendment, and this Court has twice expressed similar doubts. Thus, it is plain that the course of decision followed by the Court today entails the resolution of important and difficult issues.

The only apparent way of deciding this case without reaching those issues would be to hold that the petitioners are entitled to relief on the alternative ground advanced by them: that the respondents' conduct amounted to "state action" forbidden by the Fourteenth Amendment. However, that route is not without formidable obstacles of its own, for the opinion of the Court of Appeals makes it clear that this case differs substantially from any "state action" case previously decided by this Court. . . .

The occurrence to which I refer is the recent enactment of the Civil Rights Act of 1968. Title VIII of that Act contains comprehensive "fair housing" provisions, which by the terms of 803 will become applicable on January 1, 1969, to persons who, like the petitioners, attempt to buy houses from developers. Under those provisions, such persons will be entitled to injunctive relief and damages from developers who refuse to sell to them on account of race or color, unless the parties are able to resolve their dispute by other means. Thus, the type of relief which the petitioners seek will be available within seven months' time under the terms of a presumptively constitutional Act of Congress. In these circumstances, it seems obvious that the case has lost most of its public importance, and I believe that it would be much the wiser course for this Court to refrain from deciding it. I think it particularly unfortunate for the Court to persist in deciding this case on the basis of a highly questionable interpretation of a sweeping, century-old statute which, as the Court acknowledges, contains none of the exemptions which the Congress of our own time found it necessary to include in a statute regulating relationships so personal in nature. In effect, this Court, by its construction of 1982, has extended the coverage of federal "fair housing" laws far beyond that which Congress in its wisdom chose to provide in the Civil Rights Act of 1968. The political process now having taken hold again in this very field, I am at a loss to understand why the Court should have deemed it appropriate or, in the circumstances of this case, necessary to proceed with such precipitate and insecure strides.

Harlan's Conclusion

I am not dissuaded from my view by the circumstance that the 1968 Act was enacted after oral argument in this case, at a time when the parties and amici curiae had invested time and money in anticipation of a decision on the merits, or by the fact that the 1968 Act apparently will not entitle these petitioners to the relief which they seek. For the certiorari jurisdiction was not conferred upon this Court "merely to give the defeated party in the . . . Court of Appeals another hearing," *Magnum Co. v. Coty*, or "for the benefit of the particular litigants," *Rice v. Sioux City Cemetery*, but to decide issues, "the settlement of which is of importance to the public as distinguished from . . . the parties," *Layne & Bowler Corp. v. Western Well Works, Inc.* I deem it far more important that this Court should avoid, if possible, the decision of constitutional and unusually difficult statutory questions than that we fulfill the expectations of every litigant who appears before us. . . .

For these reasons, I would dismiss the writ of certiorari as improvidently granted. . . .

Memphis v. Greene: Violation of Constitutional Rights or Routine Burden of Citizenship?

John Paul Stevens

In Memphis v. Greene (1981), the Court was asked to decide a case that involved two bordering neighborhoods. The city of Memphis, Tennessee, closed a street that connected Hein Park, a predominantly white neighborhood, to a predominantly black neighborhood north of Hein Park. The city was asked to close the street by the citizens of Hein Park to reduce traffic and to increase safety. The citizens of the neighborhood north of Hein Park sued, holding that the road closing reduced their property values, created a barrier between white and black neighborhoods, and constituted a "badge of slavery" that directly violated the Thirteenth Amendment. John Paul Stevens wrote the majority opinion, reversing a lower court decision and ruling in favor of the city of Memphis. The opinion states that the road closing was simply a "routine burden of citizenship." Stevens was appointed to the Supreme Court on December 19, 1975.

The question presented is whether a decision by the city of Memphis to close the north end of West Drive, a street that traverses a white residential community, violated 1 of the Civil Rights Act of 1866, Rev. Stat. 1978, 42 U.S.C. 1982, or the Thirteenth Amendment to the United States Constitution. The city's action was challenged by respondents, who resided in a predominantly black area to the north. The Court of Appeals ultimately held the street closing invalid because it adversely affected respondents' ability to hold and enjoy their property. We reverse because the record does not support that holding. . . .

The closing will have some effect on both through traffic and local traffic. Prior to the closing, a significant volume of

John Paul Stevens, Majority Opinion, *Memphis v. Greene*, 1981.

traffic southbound on Springdale St. would continue south on West Drive and then—because of the location of Overton Park to the south of Hein Park—make either a right or a left turn to the next through street a few blocks away, before resuming the southerly route to the center of the city. The closing of West Drive will force this traffic to divert to the east or west before entering Hein Park, instead of when it leaves, but the closing will not make the entire route any longer. With respect to local traffic, the street closing will add some distance to the trip from Springdale St. to the entrance to Overton Park and will make access to some homes in Hein Park slightly less convenient.

The area to the north of Hein Park is predominantly black. All of the homes in Hein Park were owned by whites when the decision to close the street was made. . . .

City Approval

Thereafter on July 9, 1973, members of the Hein Park Civic Association filed with the Memphis and Shelby County Planning Commission a formal "Application to Close Streets or Alleys" seeking permission to close West Drive for 25 feet south of Jackson Ave. The application was signed by the two property owners abutting both Jackson Ave. and West Drive and all but one of the other West Drive homeowners on the block immediately south of Jackson Ave. The stated reasons for the closing were:

> "(1) Reduce flow of through traffic using subdivision streets.
>
> "(2) Increase safety to the many children who live in the subdivision and those who use the subdivision to walk to Snowden Junior High School.
>
> "(3) Reduce 'traffic pollution' in a residential area, e. g., noise, litter, interruption of community living."

After receiving the views of interested municipal departments, the County Planning Commission on November 1,

1973, recommended that the application be approved with the conditions that the applicants provide either an easement for existing and future utility company facilities or the funds to relocate existing facilities and that the closure provide clearance for fire department vehicles. . . .

Litigation

In a complaint filed against the city and various officials in the United States District Court for the Western District of Tennessee on April 1, 1974, three individuals and two civic associations, suing on behalf of a class of residents north of Jackson Ave. and west of Springdale St., alleged that the closing was unconstitutional and prayed for an injunction requiring the city to keep West Drive open for through traffic. The District Court granted a motion to dismiss, holding that the complaint, as amended, failed to allege any injury to the plaintiffs' own property or any disparate racial effect, and that they had no standing as affected property owners to raise procedural objections to the city's action.

The United States Court of Appeals for the Sixth Circuit reversed. The court first noted that "a complaint should not be dismissed for failure to state a claim unless it appears beyond doubt that the plaintiff can prove no set of facts in support of his claim which will entitle him to relief." The court concluded that respondents' complaint, fairly construed, alleged that the city had conferred certain benefits—"to wit, the privacy and quiet of an exclusive dead-end street"—on white residents that it refused to confer on similarly situated black residents. Accordingly, the court held that if respondents could prove that city officials conferred the benefit of a closed street on West Drive residents "because of their color," respondents would have a valid claim under either 42 U.S.C. 1982 or 1983. . . .

The Court of Appeals did not reject any of the District Court's findings of fact. The Court of Appeals did hold, however, that Judge [Robert] McRae had erred by limiting his focus to the issue of whether the city had granted a street closing application made by whites while denying comparable benefits to blacks. Although the Court of Appeals recognized that the reasoning of its earlier opinion could have induced such a narrow focus, and that the record supported Judge McRae's findings on this issue, the court held that the respondents need not show that the city had denied street-closing applications submitted by black neighborhoods to show a violation of 1982. Rather, the court held that respondents could demonstrate that this particular street closing was a "badge of slavery" under 1982 and the Thirteenth Amendment without reference to the equal treatment issue.

The Court of Appeals recognized that a street closing may be a legitimate and effective means of preserving the residential character of a neighborhood and protecting it from the problems caused by excessive traffic. The Court of Appeals concluded, however, that relief under 1982 was required here by the facts: (1) that the closing would benefit a white neighborhood and adversely affect blacks; (2) that a "barrier was to be erected precisely at the point of separation of these neighborhoods and would undoubtedly have the effect of limiting contact between them"; (3) that the closing was not part of a citywide plan but rather was a "unique step to protect one neighborhood from outside influences which the residents considered to be 'undesirable'"; and (4) that there was evidence of "an economic depreciation in the property values in the predominantly black residential area." Before addressing the legal issues, we consider the extent to which each of these conclusions is supported by the record and the District Court's findings.

Evidence for the Court of Appeals' Ruling

The first of the four factual predicates for the Court of Appeals' holding relates to the effect of the closing on black presidents and is squarely rooted in the District Court's findings. Judge McRae expressly found that the City Council action "will have disproportionate impact on certain black citizens." He described the traffic that will be diverted by the closing as "overwhelming black," noted that the white residents of West Drive will have less inconvenience. We must note, however, that although neither Judge McRae nor the Court of Appeals focused on the extent of the inconvenience to residents living north of Jackson Ave., the record makes it clear that such inconvenience will be minimal. A motorist southbound on Springdale St. could continue south on West Drive for only a half mile before the end of West Drive at Overton Park would necessitate a turn. Thus unless the motorist is going to Overton Park, the only effect of the street closing for traffic proceeding south will be to require a turn sooner without lengthening the entire trip or requiring any more turns. Moreover, even the motorist going to Overton Park had to make a turn from West Drive and a short drive down North Parkway to reach the entrance to the park. The entire trip from Springdale St. to the park will be slightly longer with West Drive closed, but it will not be significantly less convenient. Thus although it is correct that the motorists who will be inconvenienced by the closing are primarily black, the extent of the inconvenience is not great.

As for the Court of Appeals' second point, the court attached greater significance to the closing as a "barrier" between two neighborhoods than appears warranted by the record. The physical barrier is a curb that will not impede the passage of municipal vehicles. Moreover, because only one of the several streets entering Hein Park is closed to vehicular traffic, the other streets will provide ample access to the residences in Hein Park. The diversion of through traffic around the Hein Park residential area affects the diverted motorists, but does not support the suggestion that such diversion will limit the social or commercial contact between residents of neighboring communities.

The Court of Appeals' reference to protecting the neighborhood from "undesirable" outside influences may be read as suggesting that the court viewed the closure as motivated by the racial attitude of the residents of Hein Park. The District Court's findings do not support that view of the record. Judge McRae expressly discounted the racial composition of the traffic on West Drive in evaluating its undesirable character; he noted that "excessive traffic in any residential neighborhood has public welfare factors such as safety, noise, and litter, regardless of the race of the traffic and the neighborhood." The transcript of the City Council hearings indicates that the residents of West Drive perceived the traffic to be a problem because of the number and speed of the cars traveling down West Drive. Even if the statements of the residents of West Drive are discounted as self-serving, there is no evidence that the closing was motivated by any racially exclusionary desire. The City Council members who favored the closing expressed concerns similar to those of the West Drive residents. Those who opposed the resolution did so because they believed that a less drastic response to the traffic problems would be adequate and that the closing would create a dangerous precedent. The one witness at trial who testified that "someone" soliciting signatures for a petition favoring the closure had described the traffic on West Drive as "undesirable traffic," stated that the solicitor mentioned excess traffic and danger to children as reasons for signing. Unlike the Court of Appeals, we therefore believe that the "undesirable" character of the traffic flow must be viewed as a factor supporting, rather than undermining, the validity of the closure decision. To the extent that the Court of Appeals' opinion can be read as making a finding of discriminatory intent, the record requires us to reject that finding in favor of the District Court's contrary conclusion. Judge McRae expressly found that the respondents had not proved that the City Council had acted with discriminatory intent. App. 161.

Finally, the Court of Appeals was not justified in inferring that the closure would cause "an economic depreciation in the property values in the predominantly black residential area. . . ." The only expert testimony credited by the District Court on that issue was provided by a real estate broker called by the plaintiffs. His expert opinion, as summarized by the District Court, was that "there would not be a decrease in value experienced by property owners located to the north of West Drive because of the closure." After the witness had expressed that opinion, he admittedly speculated that some property owners to the north might be envious of the better housing that they could not afford and therefore might be less attentive to the upkeep of their own property, which in turn "could have a detrimental effect on the property values in the future." In our opinion the District Court correctly refused to find an adverse impact on black property values based on that speculation.

In summary, then, the critical facts established by the record are these: The city's decision to close West Drive was motivated by its interest in protecting the safety and tranquility of a residential neighborhood. The procedures followed in making the decision were fair and were not affected by any racial or other impermissible factors. The city has conferred a benefit on certain white property owners but there is no reason to believe that it would refuse to confer a comparable benefit on black property owners. The closing has not affected the value of property owned by black citizens, but it has caused some slight inconvenience to black motorists.

Under the Court's recent decisions in *Washington v. Davis*, and *Arlington Heights v. Metropolitan Housing Dev. Corp.*, the absence of proof of discriminatory intent forecloses any claim that the official action challenged in this case violates the Equal Protection Clause of the Fourteenth Amendment. Petitioners ask us to hold that respondents' claims under 1982 and the Thirteenth Amendment are likewise barred by the absence of proof of discriminatory purpose. We note initially that the coverage of both 1982 and the Thirteenth Amendment is significantly different from the coverage of the Fourteenth Amendment. The prohibitions of the latter apply only to official action, or, as implemented by 42 U.S.C. 1983 (1976 ed., Supp. III), to action taken under color of state law. We have squarely decided, however, that 1982 is directly applicable to private parties, *Jones v. Alfred H. Mayer Co., Runyon v. McCrary*, and it has long been settled that the Thirteenth Amendment "is not a mere prohibition of State laws establishing or upholding slavery, but an absolute declaration that slavery or involuntary servitude shall not exist in any part of the United States." [quoting the 1883] *Civil Rights Cases*. Thus, although respondents challenge official action in this case, the provisions of the law on which the challenge is based cover certain private action as well. Rather than confront prematurely the rather general question whether either 1982 or the Thirteenth Amendment requires proof of a specific unlawful purpose, we first consider the extent to which either provision applies at all to this street closing case. We of course deal first with the statutory question. . . .

As applied to this case, the threshold inquiry under 1982 must focus on the relationship between the street closing and the property interests of the respondents. As the Court of Appeals correctly noted in its first opinion, the statute would support a challenge to municipal action benefiting white property owners that would be refused to similarly situated black property owners. For official action of that kind would prevent blacks from exercising the same property rights as whites. But respondents' evidence failed to support this legal theory. Alternatively, as the Court of Appeals held in its second opinion, the statute might be violated by official action that depreciated the value of property owned by black citizens. But this record discloses no effect on the value of property owned by any member of the respondent class. Finally, the statute might be violated if the street closing severely restricted access to black homes, because blacks would then be hampered in the use of their property. Again, the record discloses no such restriction.

The injury to respondents established by the record is the requirement that one public street rather than another must be used for certain trips within the city. We need not assess the magnitude of that injury to conclude that it does not involve any impairment to the kind of property interests that we have identified as being within the reach of 1982. We therefore must consider whether the street closing violated respondents' constitutional rights. . . .

In this case respondents challenge the conferring of a benefit upon white citizens by a measure that places a burden on black citizens as an unconstitutional "badge of slavery." Relying on Justice [Hugo] Black's opinion for the Court in *Palmer v. Thompson*, the city argues that in the absence of a violation of specific enabling legislation enacted pursuant to 2 of the Thirteenth Amendment, any judicial characterization of an isolated street closing as a badge of slavery would constitute the usurpation of "a law-making power far beyond the imagination of the amendment's authors." . . .

The Thirteenth Amendment Was Not Violated

We begin our examination of respondents' Thirteenth Amendment argument by reiterating the conclusion that the record discloses no racially discriminatory motive on the part of the City Council. Instead, the record demonstrates that the interests that did motivate the Council are legitimate. Proper management of the flow of vehicular traffic within a city requires the accommodation of a variety of conflicting interests: the motorist's interest in unhindered access to his destination, the city's interest in the efficient provision of municipal services, the commercial interest in adequate parking, the residents' interest in relative quiet, and the pedestrians' interest in safety. Local governments necessarily exercise wide discretion in making the policy decisions that accommodate these interests.

In this case the city favored the interests of safety and tranquility. As a matter of constitutional law a city's power to adopt rules that will avoid anticipated traffic safety problems is the same as its power to correct those hazards that have been revealed by actual events. The decision to reduce the flow of traffic on West Drive was motivated, in part, by an interest in the safety of children walking to school. That interest is equally legitimate whether it provides support for an arguably unnecessary preventive measure or for a community's reaction to a tragic accident that adequate planning might have prevented. . . .

The interests motivating the city's action are thus sufficient to justify an adverse impact on motorists who are somewhat inconvenienced by the street closing. That inconvenience cannot be equated to an actual restraint on the liberty of black citizens that is in any sense comparable to the odious practice the Thirteenth Amendment was designed to eradicate. The argument that the closing violates the Amendment must therefore rest, not on the actual consequences of the closing, but rather on the symbolic significance of the fact that most of the drivers who will be inconvenienced by the action are black.

But the inconvenience of the drivers is a function of where they live and where they regularly drive—not a function of their race; the hazards and the inconvenience that the closing is intended to minimize are a function of the number of vehicles involved, not the race of their drivers or of the local residents. Almost any traffic regulation—whether it be a temporary detour during construction, a speed limit, a one-way street, or a no-parking sign—have a differential impact on residents of adjacent or nearby neighborhoods. Because urban neighborhoods are so frequently characterized by a common ethnic or racial heritage, a regulation's adverse impact on a particular neighborhood will often have a disparate effect on an identifiable ethnic or racial group. To regard an inevitable consequence of that kind as a form of stigma so severe as to violate the Thirteenth Amendment would trivialize the great purpose of that charter of freedom. Proper respect for the dignity of the residents of any neighborhood requires that they accept the same burdens as well as the same benefits of citizenship regardless of their racial or ethnic origin.

This case does not disclose a violation of any of the enabling legislation enacted by Congress pursuant to 2 of the Thirteenth Amendment. To decide the narrow constitutional question presented by this record we need not speculate about the sort of impact on a racial group that might be prohibited by the Amendment itself. We merely hold that the impact of the closing of West Drive on nonresidents of Hein Park is a routine burden of citizenship; it does not reflect a violation of the Thirteenth Amendment.

The judgment of the Court of Appeals is
Reversed.

Memphis v. Greene:
Road Closing Promotes
Racial Discrimination

Thurgood Marshall

In Memphis v. Greene *(1981), the dissenting opinion takes a much different stand on the case at hand than does the majority opinion. Justice Thurgood Marshall, who wrote the dissenting opinion, writes that he finds testimony from a resident who was urged to support the road closing to avoid "undesirable traffic" quite troubling. This dissenting opinion finds that the majority decision upholds racial discrimination by allowing a predominantly white neighborhood to prevent black citizens of a neighborhood to the north from traveling through in attempt to create a white "urban 'utopia.'" Marshall states that neither the Constitution nor federal law allows the city of Memphis, Tennessee, or any other city, "to carve out racial enclaves." The opinion draws attention to the racial discrimination in the United States still prevalent over one hundred years after the Civil War. Marshall was the first African American appointed to the Supreme Court. He served from June 13, 1967, to June 28, 1991.*

This case is easier than the majority makes it appear. Petitioner city of Memphis, acting at the behest of white property owners, has closed the main thoroughfare between an all-white enclave and a predominantly Negro area of the city. The stated explanation for the closing is of a sort all too familiar: "protecting the safety and tranquility of a residential neighborhood" by preventing "undesirable traffic" from entering it. Too often in our Nation's history, statements such as these have been little more than code phrases for racial discrimination. These words may still signify racial discrimina-

Thurgood Marshall, Dissenting Opinion, *Memphis v. Greene*, 1981.

tion, but apparently not, after today's decision, forbidden discrimination. The majority, purporting to rely on the evidence developed at trial, concludes that the city's stated interests are sufficient to justify erection of the barrier. Because I do not believe that either the Constitution or federal law permits a city to carve out racial enclaves I dissent. . . .

Discrimination Below the Surface

The majority treats this case as involving nothing more than a dispute over a city's race-neutral decision to place a barrier across a road. My own examination of the record suggests, however, that far more is at stake here than a simple street closing. The picture that emerges from a more careful review of the record is one of a white community, disgruntled over sharing its street with Negroes, taking legal measures to keep out the "undesirable traffic," and of a city, heedless of the harm to its Negro citizens, acquiescing in the plan.

I readily accept much of the majority's summary of the circumstances that led to this litigation. I would, however, begin by emphasizing three critical facts. First, as the District Court found, Hein Park "was developed well before World War II as an exclusive residential neighborhood for white citizens and these characteristics have been maintained." Second, the area to the north of Hein Park, like the "undesirable traffic" that Hein Park wants to keep out, is predominantly Negro. And third, the closing of West Drive stems entirely from the efforts of residents of Hein Park. Up to this point, the majority and I are in agreement. But we part company over our characterizations of the evidence developed in the course of the trial of this case. At the close of the evidence, the trial court described this as "a situation where an all white neighborhood is seeking to stop the traffic from an overwhelmingly black neighborhood from coming through their street." In the legal and factual context before us, I find that a revealing summary of the case. The majority apparently does not. . . .

The majority does not seriously dispute the first of the four facts relied on by the Court of Appeals. In fact it concedes that the trial court "clearly concluded . . . that the adverse impact on blacks was greater than on whites." The majority suggests, however, that this "impact" is limited to the "inconvenience" that will be suffered by drivers who live in the predominantly Negro area north of Hein Park and who will no longer be able to drive through the subdivision. This, says the majority, is because residents of the area north of Hein Park will still be able to get where they are going; they will just have to go a little out of their way and thus will take a little longer to complete the trip.

This analysis ignores the plain and powerful symbolic message of the "inconvenience." Many places to which residents of the area north of Hein Park would logically drive lie to the south of the subdivision. Until the closing of West Drive, the most direct route for those who lived on or near Springdale St. was straight down West Drive. Now the Negro drivers are being told in essence: "You must take the long way around because you don't live in this 'protected' white neighborhood." Negro residents of the area north of Hein Park testified at trial that this is what they thought the city was telling them by closing West Drive. Even the District Court, which granted judgment for petitioners, conceded that "[o]bviously, the black people north of [Hein Park] . . . are being told to stay out of the subdivision." In my judgment, this message constitutes a far greater adverse impact on respondents than the majority would prefer to believe.

The majority also does not challenge the Sixth Circuit's second finding, that the barrier is being erected at the point of contact of the two communities. Nor could it do so, because the fact is not really in dispute. The Court attempts instead to downplay the significance of this barrier by calling it "a curb that will not impede the passage of municipal vehicles." But that is beside the point. Respondents did not bring this suit to

Justice Thurgood Marshall was the first African American to serve on the U.S. Supreme Court. Marshall served as an associate justice from 1967 to 1991. Collection of the Supreme Court of the United States.

challenge the exclusion of municipal vehicles from Hein Park. Their goal is to preserve access for their own vehicles. But in fact, they may not even be able to preserve access for their own persons. The city is creating the barrier across West Drive by deeding public property to private landowners. Nothing will prevent the residents of Hein Park from excluding "undesirable" pedestrian as well as vehicular traffic if they so choose. What is clear is that there will be a barrier to traffic that is to be erected precisely at the point where West Drive (and thus, all-white Hein Park) ends and Springdale St. (and the mostly Negro section) begins.

The psychological effect of this barrier is likely to be significant. In his unchallenged expert testimony in the trial court, Dr. Marvin Feit, a professor of psychiatry at the University of Tennessee, predicted that the barrier between West Drive and Springdale St. will reinforce feelings about the city's "favoritism" toward whites and will "serve as a monument to racial hostility." The testimony of Negro residents and of a real estate agent familiar with the area provides powerful support for this prediction. As the District Court put it: "[Y]ou are not going to be able to convince those black people out there that they didn't do it because they were black. They are helping a white neighborhood. Now, that is a problem that somebody is going to have to live with. . . ." I cannot subscribe to the majority's apparent view that the city's erection of this "monument to racial hostility" amounts to nothing more than a "slight inconvenience." Thus, unlike the majority, I do not minimize the significance of the barrier itself in determining the harm respondents will suffer from its erection. . . .

Possible Negative Effects on the Community

The term "undesirable traffic" first entered this litigation through the trial testimony of Sarah Terry. Terry, a West Drive resident who opposed the closing, testified that she was urged to support the barrier by an individual who explained to her that "the traffic on the street was undesirable traffic." The majority apparently reads the term "undesirable" as referring to the prospect of having any traffic at all on West Drive. But the common-sense understanding of Terry's testimony must be that the word "undesirable" was meant to describe the traffic that was actually using the street, as opposed to any traffic that might use it. Of course, the traffic that was both actually using the street and would be affected by the barrier was predominantly Negro.

But Terry's testimony is not, as the majority implies, the only Arlington Heights-type evidence produced at trial. The testimony of city planning officials, for example, strongly suggests that the city deviated from its usual procedures in deciding to close West Drive. In particular, despite an unambiguous requirement that applications for street closings be signed by "all" owners of property abutting on the thoroughfare to be closed, the city here permitted this application to go through without the signature or the consent of Sarah Terry. Perhaps more important, the city gave no notice to the Negro property owners living north of Hein Park that the Planning Commission was considering an application to close West Drive. The Planning Commission held its hearing without participation by any of the affected Negro residents and it declined to let them examine the file on the West Drive closing. It gave no notice that the City Council would be considering the issue. When respondents found out about it, they sought to state their case. But the Council gave opponents of the proposal only 15 minutes, even though some members objected that that was not enough time. Furthermore, although the majority treats West Drive as just another closing, it is, according to the city official in charge of closings, the only time the city has ever closed a street for traffic control purposes. And it cannot be disputed that all parties were aware of the disparate racial impact of the erection of the barrier. The city of Memphis, moreover, has an unfortunate but very real history of racial segregation—a history that has in the past led to intercession by this Court. All these factors represent precisely the kind of evidence that we said in Arlington Heights was relevant to an inquiry into motivation. Regardless of whether this evidence is viewed as conclusive, it can hardly be stated with accuracy that "no evidence" exists.

Most important, I believe that the findings of the District Court and the record in this case fully support the Court of Appeals' conclusion that Negro property owners are likely to suffer economic harm as a result of the construction of the barrier. In attempting to demonstrate to the trial court that the closing of West Drive would adversely affect their property, respondents first introduced the testimony of H.C. Moore, a real estate agent with 17 years' experience in the field. Moore began by predicting that after West Drive was closed, Hein Park would become "more or less a Utopia within the city of Memphis," families who had left the inner city for the suburbs would probably return in order to live there, and the property values in Hein Park "would be enhanced greatly." Moore was then asked what effect the closing would have on the property values in the Springdale area. He responded: "From an economic standpoint there would not be a lessening of value in those properties in the Springdale area, but from a psychological standpoint, it would have a tendency to have a demoralizing.". . .

Surely Moore's uncontroverted expert testimony is evidence of an impairment of property values, an impairment directly traceable to the closing of West Drive. The majority dismisses this aspect of Moore's testimony as "speculation." Yet the majority has no trouble crediting Moore's brief and conclusory testimony that the immediate impact of the closing would be negligible. Unlike the majority, I am unable to dismiss so blithely the balance of his comments.

The majority also gives insufficient weight to the testimony of Dr. Feit on this point. Dr. Feit testified, based on his experience as Director of Planning for Allegheny County, Pa., that the shift in traffic patterns as a result of the closing of West Drive would lower the property values for owners living north of Hein Park. He further testified that the closing of West Drive would lead to increased hostility toward Hein Park residents and, ultimately, to increased police harassment of residents of the Springdale area. I would have thought it in-

disputable that increased police harassment of property owners must be construed as a significant impairment of their
property interests. In my view, the combined testimony of Dr.
Feit and real estate expert Moore is sufficient to demonstrate
that the closing of West Drive will cause genuine harm to the
property rights of the Negro residents of the area north of
Hein Park.

In sum, I cannot agree with the majority's suggestion that
"[t]he injury to respondents established by the record is the
requirement that one public street rather than another must
be used for certain trips within the city," and that this requirement amounts to no more than "some slight inconvenience."
Indeed, as should be clear from the foregoing, the problem is
less the closing of West Drive in particular than the establishment of racially determined districts which the closing effects.
I can only agree with the Court of Appeals, which viewed the
city's action as nothing more than "one more of the many hu-
miliations which society has historically visited" on Negro citizens. In my judgment, respondents provided ample evidence
that erection of the challenged barrier will harm them in several significant ways. Respondents are being sent a clear,
though sophisticated, message that because of their race, they
are to stay out of the all-white enclave of Hein Park and
should instead take the long way around in reaching their des-
tinations to the south. Combined with this message are the
prospects of increased police harassment and of a decline in
their property values. It is on the basis of these facts, all firmly
established by the record, that I evaluate the legal questions
presented by this case. . . .

A Violation of Statute 1982

The majority concludes that the kind of harm that 1982 was
meant to prohibit does not exist in this case, but as I have
stated, a proper reading of the record demonstrates substantial
harm to respondents' property rights as a result of the estab-

lishment of a barrier at the northern edge of Hein Park. The closing will both burden respondents' ability to enjoy their property and also depress its value, thus falling within the literal language of 1982. Even the majority concedes that "the statute might be violated by official action that depreciated the value of property owned by [Negro] citizens." I believe that that is precisely what is challenged in this case.

The legislative history of 1982 also supports my conclusion that the carving out of racial enclaves within a city is precisely the kind of injury that the statute was enacted to prevent. In *Jones v. Alfred H. Mayer Co.*, this Court discussed the legislative history of the Civil Rights Act of 1866 in some detail, and there is no need to duplicate all of that discussion here. A few examples should suffice.

When the Civil Rights Act of 1866 was introduced, both its supporters and its opponents alike recognized the revolutionary scope of its intended purpose of eliminating discrimination. . . .

The Senate of course passed the bill in spite of Senator Peter G. Van Winkle's fears, thus repudiating his view that white residents should enjoy the absolute right to close their communities to Negroes. In enacting 1982, Congress was "fully aware of the breadth of the measure it had approved." *Jones v. Alfred H. Mayer Co.* Senator James Henry Lane, a supporter of the bill, answered the arguments of Senator Van Winkle and others by explaining that the bill would prevent a white person from "invok[ing] the power of local prejudice" against a Negro. Senator Lyman Trumbull, a sponsor of the legislation, made plain that it was intended to prohibit local discriminatory customs as well as discriminatory state laws. During the House debate over the Civil Rights Act, Representative Burton C. Cook argued that without the legislation, slavery might be perpetuated "under other names and in other forms" because "[a]ny combination of men in [a Negro's] neighborhood" might join to oppress him. As we recognized in *Jones v. Alfred*

H. Mayer Co., one goal of the Reconstruction Congress in enacting the statute was to provide protection for Negroes when "white citizens . . . combined to drive them out of their communities." . . .

Indeed, until today I would have thought that a city's erection of a barrier, at the behest of a historically all-white community, to keep out predominantly Negro traffic, would have been among the least of the statute's prohibitions. Certainly I suspect that the Congress that enacted 1982 would be surprised to learn that it has no application to such a case. Even the few portions of debate that I have cited make clear that a major concern of the statute's supporters was the elimination of the effects of local prejudice on Negro residents. In my view, the evidence before us supports a strong inference that the operation of such prejudice is precisely what has led to the closing of West Drive. And against this record, the government should be required to do far more than it has here to justify an action that so obviously damages and stigmatizes a racially identifiable group of its citizens. . . .

I end, then, where I began. Given the majority's decision to characterize this case as a mere policy decision on the part of the city of Memphis to close a street for valid municipal reasons, the conclusion that it reaches follows inevitably. But the evidence in this case, combined with a dab of common sense, paints a far different picture from the one emerging from the majority's opinion. In this picture a group of white citizens has decided to act to keep Negro citizens from traveling through their urban "utopia," and the city has placed its seal of approval on the scheme. It is this action that I believe is forbidden, and it is for that reason that I dissent.

Current Debate on Slavery and Its Impact on Modern Life

America's Debt to Slaves

Jonathan Rauch

Reparations for slavery in the United States is a complex issue with the power both to divide and to bring people together. It is about not only compensation but also the federal government's accepting responsibility for crimes against humanity. Though reparations for slavery have been talked about for many years, little legislative action has been taken since 1866, when President Andrew Johnson blocked the Freedmen's Bureau Act, which would have given land to former slaves. Still, in recent years it has been the topic of discussion by groups such as the United Nations' World Conference Against Racism, the Southern Christian Leadership Conference, and the United Church of Christ and the Christian Church. In the following article, the author argues that the current reparations movement, that is focused on collective guilt and racial accountability, can be redirected to accountability of real wrongdoers to actual sufferers, the victims of school segregation. Jonathan Rauch is a senior writer and columnist for National Journal *and a frequent contributor to* Reason.

Gradually, it is dawning on mainstream America that the issue of reparations for slavery is not going away. Just recently, there was the Bush Administration's struggle to dissuade the United Nations' World Conference Against Racism—scheduled to begin on August 31 [2001] in Durban, South Africa—from putting reparations on the agenda. But there was more, much more.

In August, the Southern Christian Leadership Conference—the renowned civil rights organization once headed by the Rev. Martin Luther King Jr. and now headed by his son—

Jonathan Rauch, "Blacks Deserve Reparations—But Not for Slavery," *National Journal*, September 1, 2001. Reproduced by permission.

called for reparations. In July, the United Church of Christ and the Christian Church (Disciples of Christ)—both predominantly white, and representing more than 2 million people between them—jointly passed resolutions calling on their members to "join in active study and education on issues dealing with reparations for slavery." In June, the chairman of the New York state Assembly's black and Hispanic caucus introduced a bill that would create a commission to "quantify the debt owed" to the descendants of nearly 22,000 slaves who were denied "life, liberty, [and] compensation for their work" by the state. In May, in a two-part editorial, no less an establishment bastion than *The Philadelphia Inquirer* called for reparations, which the paper called "a long-delayed moral task."

Until lately, mainstream opinion has mostly dismissed the reparations movement with a wave of the hand. "It's a terrible idea and it's not going to happen, so let's talk about something else," has been the attitude. After all, reparations for slavery would be counterproductive, deepening and further entrenching the racial divisions that America should seek to erase. Reparations would be a blank check, because no amount would be enough and the door would be opened to compensation for every historical injustice right back to the Egyptians' enslavement of the Jews.

Above all, reparations would be fundamentally illiberal, and therefore unjust. People who have enslaved no one (and most of whose ancestors enslaved no one) would be forced to pay damages to people who were never slaves. In the dubious name of justice for groups, injustice would be done to millions of individuals.

All of those arguments are compelling. But waving aside the reparations idea is not going to work. Nor, really, should it. The wrongs were too grievous, the harms too persistent to be shrugged aside with answers such as, "We've already fixed the problem, so just be happy you're here." Opponents of

An African American man expresses his belief that steps should be taken towards reparations for slavery. AP Images.

reparations for slavery need to stop changing the subject and instead shift the debate onto ground that squares with liberal principles.

Can a reparations movement that is currently about collective guilt and racial accountability be refocused on the accountability of real wrongdoers to actual sufferers? The answer is yes. And it has been since at least 1973.

In that year, a Yale University law professor named Boris I. Bittker (now retired) published a lucid and carefully crafted little book called *The Case for Black Reparations.* He believed that reparations, not only for slavery but also for the century of Jim Crow that followed, were compelled as a matter of justice. But he also considered a variety of broad compensation schemes and conceded that all were "fraught with dangers," including the sorts of problems I mentioned above. The result, Bittker concluded, was an abiding "American dilemma."

On the way to this bleak conclusion, however, he touched upon a much different and narrower concept of reparations: reparations not for slavery but for officially segregated schools.

"A program to compensate children who were required to go to segregated schools . . . would not raise any conceptual difficulties in identifying the beneficiaries," he wrote. "Entitlement would depend exclusively on the fact that the student was assigned to a black school, regardless of his actual racial origin."

Bittker himself expressed ambivalence about this idea. He seemed to think that, for all its administrative elegance, it offered blacks too limited a portion of redress. Officially segregated schools, after all, were just a part of the picture. No doubt partly for that reason, Bittker's suggestion found no constituency.

Well, the time has come to give Bittker's idea the serious consideration it has deserved all along. For, on the merits, the case for these narrower reparations is as strong as the case for broader slavery reparations is weak.

To begin with, the people who would be compensated are the people who suffered the harm. They are easy to identify. Many of them are very much alive. It cannot be seriously disputed that they were wronged, not only educationally but morally, by being forced into separate and hardly equal schools. Moreover, the perpetrator of the injustice is not a race, a "society," or slave owners who are all long dead. The perpetrator, like the victims, is identifiable and very much alive: government.

During World War II, the U.S. government herded more than 120,000 Japanese-Americans into "internment" (concentration) camps. The internees lost an estimated $400 million in assets, of which only about 10 percent was returned. In 1988, when the government's conscience finally caught up with its past, Congress authorized a presidential apology and $20,000 in reparations to most living internees. This, of course, was just and honorable. It would be equally just and honorable—if equally belated—to do something similar for the many living Americans who were herded not into segregated housing but into segregated schools.

The practical questions are pretty easy to address. How much to pay? Enough to show genuine contrition for an outrageous injustice, but not so much as to impose an unfair burden on today's taxpayers, not many of whom ever did or would vote for segregation. Deciding in practice what would be a fair figure is what politics and legislatures were invented for.

Who should pay? The checks should be drawn on the treasuries of the states that committed the wrong, to symbolize their institutional culpability and contrition. But the costs should be covered by Congress, because most of today's Mississippians played no part in the policies of the 1950s and '60s, and because the whole country tolerated, and even conspired in, the Jim Crow system until at least 1954, when the Supreme Court ruled school segregation unconstitutional. Recompense for the evil of official segregation should be a national deed.

Proponents of broader reparations will scoff. Half a loaf, they will say, is worse than none. What about unofficial segregation? Housing and job discrimination? Separate water fountains? Slavery itself? The answer is that, in an ideal world, none of those things would ever have happened; but identifying perpetrators and victims now is impossible, even in principle, so a reparations program would inevitably pile new injustices on top of old ones. On the whole, having attended an officially segregated school is a pretty good proxy for having borne the brunt of Jim Crow. Repaying the living victims with money and an apology is both reasonable and just. That should be the focus of the reparations campaign in America.

Opponents of reparations, on the other hand, will wonder why it is necessary to dig up the rotting corpse of school segregation. Wouldn't it be better to leave history in the past? Aren't four decades of legal reforms and social progress and white guilt enough? Wouldn't a narrow reparations program just whet activists' appetite for more, more, more?

Those objections are not frivolous, but neither do they carry the day. A wrongdoer's formal apology and restitution matter, and segregation victims have never had either. Nor have they had the right to sue the states for damages. Paying the victims a decent settlement and formally saying "sorry" seems the least that government can do. Moreover, doing so would sharpen rather than blur the boundaries of accountability, by underscoring the principle that reparations should flow from actual perpetrators to identifiable victims. The effect might thus be to cap, rather than uncork, the genie's bottle of open-ended reparations for every historical wrong.

To be resolute and credible in resisting unjust reparations, Americans need to be willing to support just ones. Supplementing that moral reality is a tactical one: The surest way to expose a crummy idea is to counter it with a good idea. Paying reparations to the living victims of school segregation may or may not be something that Americans will agree to do, but it is unquestionably fair and practical should they choose to do it. And putting a fair and practical proposal on the table could, at long last, shift the whole misbegotten reparations debate onto the right track.

The Problem with Reparations

Peter Flaherty and John Carlisle

The issue of reparations for slavery has divided people since slavery was abolished by the Thirteenth Amendment in the nineteenth century. Shortly after the Civil War ended, news spread that General William Sherman had promised former slaves "40 acres and a mule apiece." However, once that promise was recanted, the federal government made no other plans for slave reparations. The debate over compensation has raged ever since. While some argue that reparations are the only way for Americans properly to apologize for their involvement in the horrors of slavery, others feel that paying reparations for crimes committed more than a century ago would be too little, too late. In the following article, Peter Flaherty and John Carlisle establish a case against reparations by explaining that compensation would do little to heal the wounds that slavery inflicted upon this country. They feel that reparations paid to distant relatives of former slaves would not only go to the wrong people but also fail to punish those responsible for slavery. Flaherty is the president of the National Legal and Policy Center (NLPC). Carlisle is the director of policy at NLPC.

A commonly heard rationale for slave reparations is that other groups were paid compensation for suffering they endured, and that therefore African Americans deserve compensation as well. Reparations advocates often cite as precedents the payments to Jews who survived the Holocaust, and to Japanese Americans placed in U.S.-run internment camps during World War II.

The experience of these groups has certainly helped provide the slave reparations movement with much of its rationale. It follows a common tradition in American politics: one group gets a government benefit, prompting another group to demand a similar benefit. . . .

Differences in Reparations Cases

But slave reparations advocates are wrong to make this argument. In the cases of Holocaust and Japanese internment reparations, the payments went to the actual victims of the wrongdoings or to the victims' immediate families, not to the descendants of victims. Slave reparations advocates, of course, never point this out when making their case. They are seriously distorting the "it's only fair" argument, since they were never actually enslaved. . . .

Holocaust reparations are the most commonly cited "precedent" among reparations advocates. West Germany's payments to Israel following World War II are frequently mentioned, as well as the more recent lawsuits by Holocaust survivors to extract payments from German companies that profited from slave labor during the Nazi era.

In 1952, West Germany began payments to Israel to help defray expenses relating to the resettlement of Holocaust survivors, and to pay selected Holocaust survivors directly. West Germany's payments to Israel were voluntary, and the money went to actual victims of the Holocaust. Initially, Israel was even hesitant to accept the reparations. During the Israeli Knesset debate over whether to accept the payments from Germany, Menachem Begin (who was later Israel's prime minister from 1977–1983) considered such payments blood money.

In the 1990s, U.S. and German negotiators agreed to establish a $5.2 billion fund to compensate people forced to work in Germany during World War II. There were an estimated 12 million people enslaved in concentration camps or

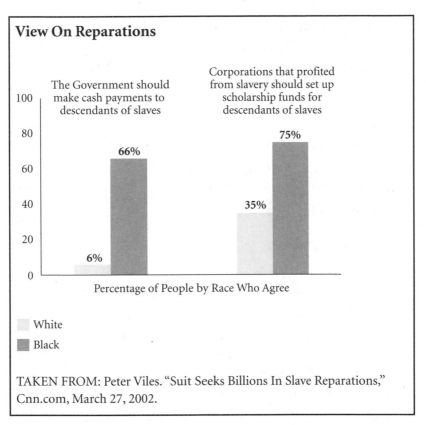

View On Reparations

The Government should make cash payments to descendants of slaves

Corporations that profited from slavery should set up scholarship funds for descendants of slaves

Percentage of People by Race Who Agree

White

Black

TAKEN FROM: Peter Viles. "Suit Seeks Billions In Slave Reparations," Cnn.com, March 27, 2002.

forced to work elsewhere—many of them non-Jews. Between 1.5 million to 2.3 million were still alive and eligible for compensation.

There also have been lawsuits against insurance companies for allegedly failing to pay Nazi-era policies, and against Swiss banks to recover assets that were deposited there during the Nazi era. (However, according to the *Times of London*, most of the dormant Swiss bank accounts belonged to wealthy non-Jewish people who had forgotten about the money.)

Slave reparations advocates also frequently cite the example of compensation paid to Japanese Americans. During World War II, about 120,000 Japanese immigrants or people of Japanese ancestry were placed in 10 internment camps, losing their freedom and, in many cases, their property. Many of them had to sell their property at far below market prices. Three years after the war, the U.S. government began to pay out $38 million in compensation to former internees. In 1988, President Reagan and Congress appropriated an additional $1.25 billion for reparations of $20,000 to each former internee.

In both the Holocaust and the Japanese internment payments, therefore, the recipients were the actual victims, or in some cases, the victims' immediate family members. The payments did not go to distant descendents. . . .

Who Really Pays?

The notion of paying recompense for what one's distant ancestor did a century and a half ago is nonsensical. Yet that is what advocates of slave reparations are demanding. Equally disturbing, the people who would receive the money are not the victims, but the great-great-great grandchildren of the victims, many of whom are much more prosperous than those who would have to pay.

But the absurdity of reparations goes much beyond that. First, only a tiny minority of Americans today has an ancestor who was a slave owner. Prior to and during the Civil War, the great majority of the population was located in the northern states where slavery was outlawed. In 1860, the population of the free states totaled about 19.5 million; the free population of the slave-owning states was 7.5 million. This means that among Americans today who had ancestors living in the United States during the slavery era, most of those ancestors lived in the non-slave owning northern states. In fact, many of those northerners were abolitionists and detested the institution of slavery.

As for the small number of Americans alive today who had ancestors living in the antebellum South, chances are those ancestors were not slave owners. Only one out of four southern whites owned slaves. Thus, only a very small percentage of contemporary Americans have direct ancestors who were slave owners. Other Americans perhaps have distant uncles or cousins who were slave owners. If reparations were mandated, this would be a case of paying recompense for an act carried out by a distant cousin of a long-deceased direct ancestor.

Most Americans Came Here After Slavery Ended

Even more significant is that the vast majority of Americans' ancestors did not even live in the United States when slavery was legal. They immigrated here after slavery was abolished. . . . There were 9.5 million people in the U.S. in 1820. Between 1820 and 1860, when slavery existed, about 5 million people immigrated to the U.S., the large majority going to the non-slave owning states and territories.

The great waves of immigration took place after the Civil War ended in 1865, particularly around 1900, as well as the most recent decade. Since 1870, more than 51 million people have immigrated to the United States.

Everyone can agree that the more-than 45 million Americans of Latin American and Asian descent are completely absolved of any complicity with U.S. slavery, since almost all of their ancestors immigrated to the U.S. long after slavery ended, most of them in recent decades. And of the very few people of Latin American or Asian origin who were U.S. citizens during the slavery era, it is safe to say that very few of them were slave owners.

What about Americans of European descent? If "guilt" is determined by one's ancestors being slave owners, then Americans of Italian, Polish, Slavic, Scandinavian and Greek descents can be sure they are completely innocent; their ancestors immigrated to the U.S. after slavery ended. Even the vast

majority of Americans of Western European origin are innocent. Their ancestors mostly came here after the Civil War as
well.

Who Really Benefits?

Another significant point is that a growing number of black
Americans do not have ancestors who were U.S. slaves. More
than a half-million Africans immigrated to the United States
in recent decades. And many if not most of those immigrants
have children, bringing the total number of African Americans
whose ancestors were not enslaved to at least a million. As-
suming reparations were paid to all blacks, a substantial number of people would be entitled to reparations whose ancestors were not even slaves.

Moreover, there were almost a million immigrants from
Haiti and Jamaica in recent decades, almost all of them black.
While their ancestors were slaves, they were not enslaved in
the U.S. Why should U.S. citizens have to pay reparations to
people whose ancestors were enslaved in another country?

But if reparations advocates get their way, that is what
would happen. To allegedly combat the injustice of slavery,
they would perpetrate an extraordinary injustice by forcing
the innocent to pay reparations to those who do even not deserve it.

Immigrant Labor as Involuntary Servitude

John Bowe

According to John Bowe, in the southeastern United States, modern-day slavery plagues immigrant communities. South Florida's agricultural labor camps, dominating and overworking desperate immigrants, can be viewed as hotbeds of slavery, he argues. Bowe explains that slave traders aid immigrants in coming to the United States in search of opportunity, and then these immigrants are forced to work for free to pay back what they "owe." While working, these immigrants are monitored constantly, threatened verbally, and often abused physically. Each year thousands of human beings are smuggled into the United States for involuntary labor. This article documents the problem of slavery for one man and his two friends. Bowe is a contributor to the New Yorker, *the* New York Times, *and* GQ, *among other magazines and newspapers.*

In many parts of the Southeast, agricultural workers are quartered in trailer camps miles from town; Immokalee's [Florida] pickers, as citrus and tomato workers are often called, live in plain sight, densely concentrated between First and Ninth Streets, close to the South Third Street pickup spot. Those who don't live there are forced either to walk a great distance twice a day or to pay extra for a ride to work. As a result, rents near the parking lot are high. The town's largest landlord, a family named Blocker, owns several hundred old shacks and mobile homes, many rusting and mildew-stained, which can rent for upward of two hundred dollars a week, a square-footage rate approaching Manhattan's. (Heat and phone service are not provided.) It isn't unusual for twelve workers to share a trailer.

John Bowe, "Nobodies: Does Slavery Exist in America?," *The New Yorker*, April 21, 2003, p. 106. Reproduced by permission of the author.

Immokalee's tomato pickers are paid as little as forty cents per bucket. A filled bucket weighs thirty-two pounds. To earn fifty dollars in a day, an Immokalee picker must harvest two tons of tomatoes, or a hundred and twenty-five buckets.

Orange- and grapefruit-picking pay slightly better, but the hours are longer. To get to the fruit, pickers must climb twelve-to-eighteen-foot-high ladders, propped on soggy soil, then reach deep into thorny branches, thrusting both hands among pesticide-coated leaves before twisting the fruit from its stem and rapidly stuffing it into a shoulder-slung *moral*, or pick sack. (Grove owners post guards in their fields to make sure that the workers do not harm the trees.) A full sack weighs about a hundred pounds; it takes ten sacks—about two thousand oranges—to fill a *baño*, a bin the size of a large wading pool. Each bin earns the worker a *ficha*, or token, redeemable for about seven dollars. An average worker in a decent field can fill six, seven, maybe eight bins a day. After a rain, though, or in an aging field with overgrown trees, the same picker might work an entire day and fill only three bins.

Migrant workers are usually employed by labor contractors, who provide crews to tend and harvest crops for local farmers, or growers, as they're more commonly known. Contractors oversee workers in groups ranging in size from a dozen to many hundreds, and accompany the workers as they travel with the seasons. They can exert near-absolute control over their workers' lives; besides handling the payroll and deducting taxes, they are frequently the sole source of the workers' food and housing, which, in addition to the ride to and from the fields, they provide for a fee. . . .

A Modern Form of Slavery

All these factors combine to create, in South Florida, what a Justice Department official calls "ground zero for modern slavery." The area has seen six cases of involuntary servitude successfully prosecuted in the past six years. . . .

In February of 2001, Adan Ortiz decided [with two friends] to leave his home in the Mexican state of Campeche, on the Yucatán Peninsula, where he lived with his wife and six children in a one-room straw hut, to look for a job in the United States. . . .

On March 13th, more than three weeks after leaving home, the men reached their destination: Lake Placid, a low-lying town in the swamps of South Florida, about sixty miles north of Immokalee. The van stopped in front of a Mexican grocery store named La Guadalupana, and the passengers were ordered to stay put while El Chaparro got out and talked to two labor contractors, who were later identified to the migrants by their nicknames, Nino and El Diablo. . . .

Ortiz recalls that when he and his friends first met the new bosses "Señor Nino asked if we had someone to pay El Chaparro for our ride." Ortiz says that Nino shoved a phone in his face, knowing, of course, that the new arrivals had no one to call. Then, according to Ortiz, Nino said, "Well, O.K., we'll pay for you." The workers saw Nino write out a check to El Chaparro. They were told that the bosses had paid a thousand dollars for each of them. . . .

Nino didn't make anyone sign a contract. Instead, he simply warned his new recruits, "You'll have to pay us back. And the work is very hard." Nino then added a final detail, according to Ortiz: "He told us that if anyone took off before paying he'd beat the f--- out of us. He didn't say it like he was joking." At that point, seeking another job wasn't an option. As Ortiz explained, "I couldn't have gone elsewhere. I owed the money to them. If I refused, what was I going to do?" . . .

Ortiz, Hernandez, and Sanchez spent the next month working for the Ramoses, eight to twelve hours a day, six or seven days a week. Every Friday after work, Nino or El Diablo would pull up to the groves or in front of La Guadalupana (which was owned by Alicia Barajas) in a Ford F-250 pickup truck, holding a large sack full of money. After charging workers a check-cashing fee, the brothers then garnisheed for rent, food, work equipment, the ride from Arizona, and daily transportation to and from the fields. Whatever remained was usually spent on food at La Guadalupana. The three friends and their fellow-laborers barely broke even.

They were also under constant surveillance. La Piñita was only a few yards away from Highway 27, which runs through the citrus belt west of Lake Okeechobee. One day, when Hernandez and another worker tried to telephone their wives from a nearby Kash n' Karry convenience store, El Diablo pulled up behind them, asked whom they were calling, and pointedly offered them a ride home. When the Ramos brothers weren't around, workers were watched by relatives and supervisors carrying cell phones who lived in the barracks and patrolled the surrounding area. Ortiz recalled being told by one supervisor, "If you want to leave, go ahead. But I'll call the bosses, and they'll feed you to the alligators." The supervisor pointed to a lake behind La Piñita and said, "They haven't eaten for a while." For the newcomers, life in the United States wasn't quite what they had expected. Sanchez later recalled, "All of a sudden, you realize you're completely in their pockets." . . .

Making a Difficult Case

In the past two decades, according to the United States Department of Labor, farm receipts from fruit and vegetable sales have nearly doubled. Between 1989 and 1998, however, wages paid to farmworkers declined, dropping from $6.89 to $6.18 per hour. The national median annual income for farmworkers is $7,500. A University of Florida survey found that the average income for Immokalee farmworkers is even lower—in 1998, just $6,574.

According to the Department of Justice, the number of prosecutions of human-trafficking cases throughout the country has tripled in the past three years; there are currently [in

2003] a hundred and twenty-five investigations of such cases under way. Typically, these cases take years to pursue, and convictions with meaningful sentences are difficult to obtain. An often insuperable obstacle is the agricultural workers' mistrust of enforcement agents. Michael Baron, of the Border Patrol, says, "Workers see us and think we're here to pick them up and deport them. They don't give us the time of day." Prosecutors cite an additional hurdle: witnesses travelling from state to state without telephones are difficult to reach, much less schedule for depositions and trials.

For this reason, the Justice Department has been relying on an advocacy group called the Coalition of Immokalee Workers. The coalition has been instrumental in five of South Florida's slavery prosecutions, uncovering and investigating abusive employers, locating transient witnesses, and encouraging them to overcome their fears of testifying against former captors. While other farmworkers'-rights organizations offer health care or legal representation, the coalition holds weekly meetings, conducts weekend "leadership trainings," makes outreach trips throughout the southeastern states, stages hunger strikes, and has launched a boycott of Taco Bell, in an effort to raise wages for tomato pickers working in what it calls "sweatshop-like conditions." . . .

According to [Laura] Germino [who helped start the coalition], modern slavery exists not because today's workers are immigrants or because some of them don't have papers but because agriculture has always managed to sidestep the labor rules that are imposed upon other industries. When the federal minimum-wage law was enacted, in 1938, farmworkers were excluded from its provisions, and remained so for nearly thirty years. Even today, farmworkers, unlike other hourly workers, are denied the right to overtime pay. In many states, they're excluded from workers' compensation and unemployment benefits. Farmworkers receive no medical insurance or sick leave, and are denied the right to organize. Germino said,

"There's no other industry in America where employers have as much power over their employees."

Five of South Florida's six recent slavery cases involve workers picking tomatoes or citrus. Taco Bell buys millions of pounds of tomatoes each year through local packing companies. According to Jonathan Blum, vice-president for public relations of YUM, the parent of Taco Bell, the company does not divulge the names of its suppliers, and has refused requests from the coalition for help in negotiating with local growers for better pay and conditions. "It's a labor dispute between a company that's unrelated to Taco Bell and its workers," Blum told me. "We don't believe it's our place to get involved in another company's labor dispute involving its employees." As for the relation between slavery in South Florida and his company's chalupas, Blum said, "My gosh, I'm sorry, it's heinous, but I don't think it has anything to do with us."

Citrus-industry representatives similarly maintain that because they don't own or operate the groves the problem of slavery is not their responsibility. A spokesperson for Tropicana, one of whose largest suppliers employed the Ramoses, assured me, "We do our very best to make sure our growers operate at the highest ethical standards. If labor abuses came to our attention, we would terminate our contract with that grower." When I asked her if that had ever occurred, she checked and reported back that, as it happened, no contract had ever been terminated.

The State Department estimates that every year smugglers bring into this country illegally some fifty thousand women and children, either involuntarily or under false pretenses. In 2000, the department, alarmed by the increase in human trafficking, worked with allies in Congress to pass the Trafficking Victims Protection Act. Essentially, it proposed a federal felony charge for involuntary servitude, updating the Thirteenth Amendment's prohibition of slavery to take into account the forms of debt peonage and psychological coercion that characterize modern slavery. Early drafts of the bill provided a prison sentence for any person who profits, "knowing, or having reason to know," that a worker will be subject to involuntary servitude. According to people involved in the process, by the time the bill left Congress the provisions regarding "knowing, or having reason to know" had been stripped, largely at the insistence of Senator Orrin Hatch, of Utah, who threatened to hold up the bill in committee indefinitely. As a result, the penalties for involuntary servitude apply virtually only to labor contractors—the lowest rung of employers in the long chain that brings produce from the field to the table.

In one of the most vicious operations uncovered thus far by the coalition, Miguel Flores, of La Belle, Florida, and Sebastian Gomez, of Immokalee, were arrested seven years ago on charges of extortion and slavery. Flores, a contractor, controlled hundreds of workers in agricultural camps between Florida and North Carolina, and charged his laborers exorbitant prices for food, insuring continued indebtedness. Workers were forced to work six days a week, netting at most fifteen dollars a day. According to one Flores victim, female camp residents were raped, and gunfire was often used by guards to keep order. Flores warned his workers that if they ever spoke about their experiences he would cut out their tongues. The coalition, however, located a dozen witnesses, and, working with Michael Baron and other officials, encouraged them to testify. Flores and Gomez are now spending fifteen years in a federal prison.

In April of 1998, Rogerio Cadena and fifteen others, including several relatives, were charged with smuggling twenty women and girls, some as young as fourteen, into the United States from Mexico with promises of jobs in housekeeping, landscaping, and child care. The women were made to pay a smuggling fee of more than two thousand dollars each and held in sexual slavery in trailer-home brothels in South Florida and the Carolinas.

Federal officials said the brothels' clients were usually agricultural workers, who were charged twenty dollars by the brothel operators, or *ticketeros*. The women were required to perform between fifteen and twenty-five sexual acts per day, and received three dollars for each one. The women were told that they would be free to go once they paid off their debts, but those debts never seemed to decrease. "At the end of the night, I turned in the condom wrappers," one woman testified in a Senate hearing. "Each wrapper represented a supposed deduction from my smuggling fee. We tried to keep our own records, but the bosses destroyed them. We were never sure what we owed."

Beatings and threats of reprisals against their families in Mexico were used to keep the women in line. Several who attempted to escape were hunted down and returned to the brothels, and were punished with rape and further confinement. Victims who became pregnant were forced to have abortions and to return to work within weeks; the cost of the abortion was added to their debt. Although six of Cadena's accomplices pleaded guilty in the case, nine others managed to run away and slip back across the border. The victims were worried about the risks of testifying until Julia Gabriel, a witness in the Flores case who later became a coalition member, met with them and urged them to stand up for themselves.

According to Leon Rodriguez, a former prosecutor with the Justice Department's Civil Rights Division who helped prosecute the Flores case, the number of women in sexual-slavery rings around the country is not in the hundreds but in the thousands. "You can't just look at these as isolated labor violations or sex crimes," he said. "What you get with agriculture is a pattern of exploitation that can be understood only as a system of human-rights abuses."

Working to End the Abuse

The Coalition of Immokalee Workers initially learned about the Ramoses' slavery operation through its worker network.

Germino recalled, "We had this one woman who sells cassettes out of her van, a peddler. She came into the office out of the blue and said, 'You guys really need to go look at what's going on up there in Lake Placid.' This is like in '99 or something. She left a number. Eventually, we called her, but her number was out of order. Then we heard something from a van driver." *Servicios de transporte* serve the migrant community throughout the country; tickets are sold primarily through grocery and dry goods stores that cater to workers. According to Germino, the van driver, a coalition member, told her, "They've got some deal going on up there in Lake Placid, where it's pretty out of control. They're buying and selling people, and people aren't free to leave.". . .

To find out more about the Ramoses' operation, a nineteen-year-old Guatemalan coalition member named Romeo Ramirez volunteered to go undercover. He approached the Ramoses, asked for a job, and worked for them, observing firsthand the conditions in the fields and at La Piñita, where Mario Sanchez, Adan Ortiz, and Rafael Solis Hernandez were being held against their will.

What Ramirez reported confirmed the rumors of involuntary servitude, and on Palm Sunday, 2001, several coalition members visited the workers at La Piñita and asked about their situation: Did they know that in America even debtors can work anywhere they wish? Were they free to come and go as they pleased? Open conversation was impossible, because of the guards, but a worker whispered to Germino, "We're not free here. We can't go anywhere we want because we're not free to leave." Germino slipped him a card with the coalition's phone number.

The following Saturday, Hernandez sneaked out of the barracks to the Kash n' Karry and called the coalition. An escape plan was set for later that evening. Around midday, though, Nino showed up at La Piñita in a rage. A worker had escaped the night before. Nino swore and shouted at the remaining workers that if anyone else left he would hunt them down and kill them.

For the three friends, it was too late to change their plan. Ortiz recalled his feelings about entrusting his safety to the strangers who had promised to help him. "We were shivering," he said. "We were shaking. Because we thought maybe they are his people, too, and they might kill us. But then we thought, Oh, well. If we're going to die anyway, better to die trying to escape." As a final precaution, Ortiz tucked a pair of scissors into his boots. Then the three men went into the yard outside the barracks, trying to act as if they were simply passing the time.

Around sunset, a white Mercury Grand Marquis with tinted windows pulled off Highway 27, a short distance from La Piñita. Lucas Benitez emerged and raised the hood, as if checking an overheated radiator. From the balcony of a nearby hotel, Asbed and Germino signalled that the coast was clear.

Ortiz, Sanchez, and Hernandez sat on a railroad tie at the camp's edge, near the highway debating what they were about to do. Then, leaving all their belongings, including their Mexican documents, behind, they walked slowly toward the roadside. As they neared the Grand Marquis, they suddenly began sprinting, and jumped into the back seat as Benitez slammed the hood closed, get behind the wheel, and gunned the car down the road. The passengers kept their heads out of view until they were twenty miles away.

Now that witnesses were available, the government finally became involved. Two days after the escape, F.B.I. agents interviewed the freed workers. The Ramoses, along with their cousin Jose Luis, were arrested and eventually charged with conspiracy, extortion, and possession of firearms.

The Ramos trial took place in the U.S. District Court for the Southern District of Florida, in Fort Pierce, a hundred miles up the coast from Miami, and lasted three weeks. Of the three attorneys defending the Ramoses, the lead strategist was Joaquin Perez, a handsome Miami Cuban in his fifties with thoughtful eyes, a full head of lightly gelled black hair, and a flair for stylish suits. Perez, who has represented Carlos Castano, the head of the Colombian paramilitaries, spends most of his time defending high-level drug cases. He told me that he wouldn't make as much money representing Ramiro Ramos as he normally made, but he found the case engaging anyway. "I mean, slavery—it's exciting, right? It's sort of sensational."

Perez's defense argument was simple: Florida agriculture is an unsavory world. Why should the Ramoses be the only ones on the stand? What about the companies that hired them? The case would never even have come to trial, he said, if not for the Feds' need to seem proactive, the coalition's desire to make a name for itself, and the pickers' desperation for working papers, which they would receive in return for testifying.

The prosecution presented testimony from Department of Labor and Social Security Administration employees confirming that, of six hundred and eighty Social Security numbers used by the Ramoses for payroll, only ten were legitimate. Jose Martinez, the van-service owner, described being pistol-whipped by the Ramoses the night of the van attack—use of a deadly weapon and interference with interstate commerce. Ortiz, Hernandez, and Sanchez testified that they had been held and forced to work against their will. . . .

After a day and a half of deliberation, the jury found the Ramoses guilty. On November 20th, Juan and Ramiro were sentenced to twelve years; their cousin Jose Luis was sentenced to ten. At the sentencing, Judge Moore, without excusing the Ramoses' actions, gently admonished the prosecutors not to devote the lion's share of their resources to the "occasional case that we see from time to time that this case represents" but, rather, to recognize that "others at a higher level of the fruit picking industry seem complicit in one way or another with how these activities occur."

Since leaving the Ramoses' employ, Ortiz, Hernandez, and Sanchez have worked in Georgia, South Carolina, Missouri, Indiana, and Kentucky. Today, they live together in Florida, in a working-class neighborhood lined with palm trees and live oaks, sharing a tidy one-bedroom apartment with no phone.

Combating Modern-Day Slavery

John R. Miller

John R. Miller, the director of the State Department's Office to Monitor and Combat Trafficking in Persons, explains that slavery is alive and well in modern society. Miller notes that after the trade of arms and drugs, human trafficking is one of the largest sources of income for organized crime throughout the world. He describes how U.S. policies condemning these practices can help victims of human trafficking and slavery worldwide. Such policies, he maintains, not only increase awareness of the current problem of slavery but also strengthen laws that aid in the prosecution of traffickers and provide assistance to victims.

Do U.S. sanctions move other countries toward progress on human rights? Of one thing I am sure: On the emerging human rights issue of the 21st century—modern-day slavery—the threat of cutting U.S. aid has brought forth efforts that will free thousands from bondage.

That slavery exists as we enter 2004 may shock many. Nonetheless, slavery in many forms, particularly sex and forced labor, reaches into almost every country. Sex slavery affects thousands of women and children and has caused trafficking in human beings to become the third-largest source of money for organized crime, after the drug and arms trades. That grim reality motivated President [George W.] Bush this fall to become the first world leader to raise the slavery issue at the U.N. General Assembly. He called for new international efforts to fight the slave trade and pledged to almost double U.S. resources devoted to this cause.

The U.S. government estimates that 800,000 to 900,000 men, women and children are trafficked across international

"Slavery in 2004." U.S. Department of State, January 1, 2004, p. A25.

borders every year, including 18,000 to 20,000 into the United States. Some estimate total worldwide slavery to be in the millions.

In September I visited a number of countries to meet with the human beings behind such numbers. If you talk with Sasha, a former sex slave in Amsterdam, or with Lord, a former factory slave in Bangkok, you quickly understand the toll this takes on individual bodies and spirits. The story that one victim, Maria, told Congress a few years ago is typical. Lured with the hope of a restaurant job from Vera Cruz, Mexico, and trafficked through Texas, Maria was finally delivered to a brothel in Florida. There she resisted but—frightened, threatened, beaten and raped in a strange land—she succumbed and "worked" to pay off the debts that traffickers claimed she owed them.

Cases such as hers and the urgings of faith-based and feminist organizations led Congress to pass legislation that not only strengthened U.S. prosecution of traffickers and assistance to victims but also mandated the State Department to report on slavery and the slave trade around the world.

Political Progress

And here we see how the threat of economic penalties has started to play a crucial role. For the first two years the law was in effect, there were zero consequences. But this year, Congress provided that countries rated by the State Department as having made no significant efforts be faced with the potential loss of U.S. military aid, educational and cultural assistance, and support from the World Bank and International Monetary Fund.

In the three months before the slavery report came out this past June, my office saw more progress in some countries than in the previous two years. Laws against trafficking in persons were passed in places from the Philippines to Haiti.

Burkina Faso. Victims were rescued and massive arrests of traffickers were made in Cambodia and Serbia.

The U.S. law provided that for those countries poorly rated in this year's report, there would be a three-month period to make antislavery efforts. In 10 countries, including military allies of the United States, there was a flurry of activity.

Turkey set up and implemented new screening procedures that recognized 200 victims. Georgia appointed special officers with responsibility for trafficking and started broadcasting hotline numbers for victims on national television. The Dominican Republic launched a national educational billboard campaign and set up a national anti-trafficking police unit with special prosecutors. In these and other countries there were numerous arrests and prosecutions.

Of course not all these actions resulted from the threat of aid cuts. Many government officials, finally recognizing the enormity of the human crises, wanted to act. Some undoubtedly were embarrassed by the State Department's report. Strenuous efforts by diplomats in many U.S. embassies were crucial.

Continuing to Fight Slavery

We continue, however, to face the problem that many countries' economies have links to slavery. Corrupt and complicit police pose a challenge in many nations. And there is the difficulty of trying to fight diseases such as HIV-AIDS at the same time we are fighting the sex trafficking that causes so much of that disease.

To meet these challenges we need support and action at home and antislavery allies abroad. But we also need the willingness to impose economic penalties that give antislavery laws and diplomacy meaning.

Slavery in U.S. Prisons

Kim Gilmore

In this article, Kim Gilmore discusses the problem of modern-day slavery as related to America's prisons, which often contain disproportionate numbers of minority inmates. She argues that prison sentences are often steeper for minorities, who are more likely to be convicted of their crimes than are nonminorities. Sentences also seem to be more serious for nonviolent, drug-related offenses—the types of crimes often associated with low-income, inner-city convicts, she says. Gilmore points out that these sentences sometimes involve mandatory hard labor and a culture of violence and exploitation, which many people associate with slavery. Gilmore is a member of Critical Resistance East, a group that seeks to address the growth of prisons.

In the year 2000, as the punishment industry becomes a leading employer and producer for the U.S. "state," and as private prison and "security" corporations bargain to control the profits of this traffic in human unfreedom, the analogies between slavery and prison abound. This year the U.S. prison population cascaded past 2,000,000, with millions more under the jurisdiction of the criminal justice system in local jails awaiting trial, in INS [Immigration and Naturalization Services] prisons awaiting deportation, or in their homes linked with criminal justice authorities through ankle bracelets that track their every move. Recent studies of the prison boom stress the persistent disparities in sentencing according to race—prison populations continue to be disproportionately African American and Latino. With longer sentences being imposed for nonviolent drug offenses, with aggressive campaigns aimed at criminalizing young people, and with the

Kim Gilmore, "Slavery and Prison—Understanding the Connections," *Social Justice*, vol. 27, no. 3, Fall 2000, p. 195. Reproduced by permission.

growing number of children left orphaned by the criminal justice system, the carceral reach of the state and private corporations resonates with the history of slavery and marks a level of human bondage unparalleled in the 20th century.

Historical Precedent

Scholars and activists have plunged into an examination of the historical origins of racialized slavery as a coercive labor form and social system in an attempt to explain the huge increase in mass incarceration in the U.S. since the end of World War II. Drawing these links has been important in explaining the relationship between racism and criminalization after emancipation, and in connecting the rise of industrial and mechanized labor to the destructive effects of deindustrialization and globalization. The point of retracing this history is not to argue that prisons have been a direct outgrowth of slavery, but to interrogate the persistent connections between racism and the global economy. Mass imprisonment on the level seen in the U.S. in the 20th century occupies a phase along the spectrum of unfree labor related to, yet distinct from, chattel slavery. As many scholars of the punishment industry have shown, regardless of the labor prisoners do to service the larger economy (either private or public), prisons increasingly function in the U.S. economy as answers to the devastation unleashed by the dual forces of Reaganomics [President Ronald Reagan's economic policies] and the globalization of capital. The immediate post-emancipation period is a key place to start in outlining the investment of the U.S. state in this trade in humanity.

Related to the above is the growth of new abolitionist movements whose goals are the elimination of mass imprisonment as a method of treatment for addiction and mental illness, as an economic ameliorative, and as a method of social control—what one scholar [Loïc Wacquant] has termed "the carceral management of poverty". The connections between slavery and imprisonment have been used by abolitionists as an historical explanation and as part of a radical political strategy that questions the feasibility of "reform" as an appropriate response to prison expansion. As a leader in the creation of this new abolitionist movement, Angela Davis has written, "I choose the word 'abolitionist' deliberately. The 13th Amendment, when it abolished slavery, did so except for convicts. Through the prison system, the vestiges of slavery have persisted. It thus makes sense to use a word that has this historical resonance." Though some 20th-century abolitionist movements connect themselves expressly with the tradition of 19th-century abolitionists and antislavery advocates, abolitionism as defined here is the conglomerate of many local movements that express abolitionist aims indirectly through challenging the fundamental methods of the prison-industrial complex—mandatory minimum sentences, harsh penalties for nonviolent drug offenses, and the continuous construction of prisons that goes on regardless of crime rates. Although a fully conceptualized abolitionism is starting to emerge, it may be useful to outline some of the historical antecedents to current anti-prison and antiracist movements. . . .

The Connections Between Slavery and Prison

Studies of the relationship between slavery and mass imprisonment have a long history in the United States and internationally. This article will discuss some of the connections activist groups have made between the legacy of slavery and the prison expansion of the last several decades, starting with a brief outline of some of the historical scholarship on the convict lease program, the Black Codes, and later, Jim Crow. Tracing this history and the relationship between slavery and prison expansion can help inform current efforts toward prison abolition and provide a context for moving beyond reforms that have usually boosted the carceral state through a rejuvenation of the prison system, rather than clearing a path for true liberation and transformation.

From the vantage point of post-slavery emancipation, it seemed like the possibility of genuine freedom and democracy for freed slaves was a reality in the making. Although the roots of 19th-century abolitionism were varied, the popular understanding is that it was a middle-class movement led by whites and a few ex-slaves. In reality, much of the scholarship on abolitionism conflicts with this limited conception of the coalitions that powered the move to end slavery. Whether rushing over Union lines to fight against the Confederacy, planning slave revolts, or resisting slavery through countless individual acts, freed blacks and slaves challenged the foundations of a labor and social system based on racialized slavery. Anti-slavery efforts spearheaded by slaves pushed emancipation as they refused to accept the terms of gradual emancipation. African-American slaves and anti-slavery activists sought not only the abolition of slavery as a labor form, but also a broader realization of slaves' dreams of freedom, alive despite hundreds of years of violence and coerced labor. These visions of freedom rarely conformed to the narrowly articulated parameters defined in the Constitution; yet to make their ideas plausible to the state, freed slaves often had to frame their arguments for freedom in the language and categories constructed by the formal state. Although the creation of African-American free communities and institutions during Reconstruction were almost immediately threatened by new configurations of white power and supremacy, freed slaves continued to exercise their right to vote and hold office in order to enact their own plans for education, land ownership, and self-determination. This incomplete transformation was cut short by vigilante justice and racialized violence, as well as by the state-sponsored criminalization of African Americans.

In the past decade, several influential studies of this period have revealed the relationship between emancipation, the 13th

Amendment, and convict lease program. Built into the 13th Amendment was state authorization to use prison labor as a bridge between slavery and paid work. Slavery was abolished "except as a punishment for crime." This stipulation provided the intellectual and legal mechanisms to enable the state to use "unfree" labor by leasing prisoners to local businesses and corporations desperate to rebuild the South's infrastructure. During this period, white "Redeemers"—white planters, small farmers, and political leaders—set out to rebuild the preemancipation racial order by enacting laws that restricted black access to political representation and by creating Black Codes that, among other things, increased the penalties for crimes such as vagrancy, loitering, and public drunkenness. As African Americans continued the process of building schools, churches, and social organizations, and vigorously fought for political participation, a broad coalition of Redeemers used informal and state-sponsored forms of violence and repression to roll back the gains made during Reconstruction. Thus, mass imprisonment was employed as a means of coercing resistant freed slaves into becoming wage laborers. Prison populations soared during this period, enabling the state to play a critical role in mediating the brutal terms of negotiation between capitalism and the spectrum of unfree labor. The transition from slave-based agriculture to industrial economies thrust ex-slaves and "unskilled" laborers into new labor arrangements that left them vulnerable to depressed, resistant white workers or pushed them outside the labor market completely.

The transfer of power to the state signaled by the 13th Amendment profoundly reshaped the political landscape along with emancipation. By empowering the state to regulate relationships between private individuals, the state also gained the ability to determine the contours of freedom and unfreedom. The expansion of state jurisdiction thus had the dual effect of establishing legal rights for African Americans while paving the way for new, state-maintained structures of racism. Convict labor became increasingly racialized: it was assumed that blacks were more suitable for hard physical labor on Southern prison farms and on corporate railroad and construction company projects. Contrary to popular representations of chain gang labor, not only black men, but also black women were forced to work on the lines and on hard labor projects, revealing how the slave order was being mirrored in the emerging punishment system. This mimicking of the slave system structure in the post-emancipation prison system, particularly in the South, suggested a belief that the performance of antebellum culture could bring the slave system back to life. In Northern prisons, which had historically been structured around industrial rather than agricultural labor, racially based divisions were sharpened after emancipation as well. African Americans were criminalized for committing Black Code–type crimes and often were subject to tougher sentences than those imposed upon whites convicted of similar crimes.

Even though the efforts of ex-slaves and other abolitionists made it impossible to reinstall legalized chattel slavery, racialized labor arrangements persisted in the form of convict labor. Convict labor built the post-Civil War infrastructure in the U.S., not just in the South but also throughout the U.S., and the struggle to determine how free unfree labor would be continued. Labor unions, which had always been skeptical about prison labor, aggressively lobbied against the leasing of convicts to private corporations. Throughout the Depression years, unionists made it clear that an expanded use of prison labor would further imperil an already overfull work force and intervene in "free markets" in ways that threatened the stability of capitalism and laid bare its most excessive failures. Slowly, prisons and jails solved this problem by developing a "state-use" system in which prison labor was used solely for state projects. This solution eliminated the competition between convict labor and union labor, while still enabling convicts to offset their cost to the state. The Prison Industries Re-organization Administration (PIRA), a New Deal project, conducted a massive study of prison labor in all 50 states and concluded by outlining this new state-use system. Citing over-crowding and inadequate facilities, the PIRA recommended the expansion of the prison system and the construction of new prisons in almost every state. No clear statistics dem-onstrate that "crime," particularly violent crime, had increased during this period. Moreover, many of those who ended up in prison were criminalized for crimes stemming from unem-ployment, suggesting that if the state had had a handle on unemployment, there may not have been a need for more prisons. Thus, the PIRA embodied one of the many contradic-tions embedded in the "New Deal state"—its inability (or unwillingness) to deal with its overabundance of labor. Thus, the PIRA, together with a racialized labor system that had roots in the slave system, cleared the path for the prison–industrial complex that has flourished in the post–World War II period.

The Fight Against Prison Slavery

Given the links between the legacy of slavery and mass im-prisonment of people of color in the U.S., it might be useful to examine how a few previous prison abolition movements positioned themselves in relation to this history. These groups were often led by Quakers or inspired by the Quaker aboli-tionists of the 19th century. One such group, the Committee to Abolish Prison Slavery (CAPS), was active in the late 1970s and early 1980s and saw the abolition of mass imprisonment as the key to completing the partial emancipation signaled by the 13th Amendment. According to CAPS, which produced *Prison Slavery*, their collaboratively authored book, the tri-umph of emancipation was not a total victory since the 13th Amendment legalized penal servitude as punishment for par-ticular crimes, a stipulation that was incorporated into many

For some African Americans, slavery has left a legacy in modern America from which it can be hard to break free. © Ked Kashi/Corbis.

state constitutions. *Prison Slavery* cites the significant 1871 court ruling from *Ruffin v. Commonwealth*. This landmark Virginia case—revealingly argued using the language of slavery—set a precedent for state control of inmate bodies and labor. . . .

When *Prison Slavery* was published in 1982, many states still had clauses in their constitutions that deemed slavery and indentured servitude legal punishments or had no proviso about the legality or illegality of prison enslavement (some states eliminated any reference to slavery in the middle decades of this century). Since this 13th Amendment provision was, for CAPS, the legal cornerstone codifying prison slavery, they proposed a "new abolitionism" that would make the elimination of these clauses from all constitutions its goal. Their abolitionist strategies also included education campaigns to inform the public about prison conditions, an issue typically relegated to the sidelines of an individual's physical and psychic landscapes. The group also advocated boycotting consumer products made by prison labor, supporting alternatives to imprisonment, and working toward an acknowledgement of the class-based exploitation inherent in mass imprisonment. By circulating petitions that would amend state punishment clauses, CAPS created alliances between prisoners on the inside and activists on the outside. They learned of the brutalities that often occurred behind prison walls through testimonies from inmates who had developed their own analyses of prison system injustices, but frequently found themselves confined by the limited resources available to them, or constrained by criminal justice administrators and guards who threatened prisoners with violence for expressing their views and working for change.

Like CAPS, the Prison Research Education Action Project (PREAP) saw the abolition of prisons as the only avenue for real change, for reform movements generally succeeded only in temporarily improving prison conditions rather than questioning the very efficacy of long-term punishment. In their handbook for change, Instead of Prisons, PREAP catalogued the general sentiment of the prison abolition movement of the 1970s—espoused by elected officials, inmates, excons, former prison administrators, and inmate advocates—that evidence revealed that incarceration was hardly a deterrent to crime and that it actually tended to exacerbate crime. The early 1970s marked the onset of new drug laws and sentencing guidelines, such as the Rockefeller drug laws in New York that provided the legal justification for prison expansion throughout the U.S. During the first half of the 1970s, however, a prisoners' rights revolution was going on, in which prisoners all over the U.S. were filing individual and class action lawsuit s that challenged the constitutionality of the conditions existing within U.S. prisons, including unchecked violence and inhumane working situations. Legal theorists— using evidence that attempts of reform movements to improve conditions inside prisons continually fell short and failed to protect inmates from cruel and unusual punishment—argued that the state's goal should be the gradual elimination of long-term sentences for drug offenders and other nonviolent prisoners. While these lawsuits brought abolitionist views into the courts, groups like PREAP were learning to balance legal strategies for change with other tactics. Such tactics included gathering acknowledgements from different arenas that mass imprisonment was failing—failing to address the problems of violence, failing to rehabilitate, and failing to provide anything but a destructive response to issues of racism, unemployment, and deindustrialization. . . .

A Need for National Attention

From the late 1960s to the mid-1970s, the prisoners' rights movement helped to bring the violence and disorder that prevailed in U.S. prisons to the forefront of public consciousness. Previous to the landmark prisoners' rights cases of the 1960s and 1970s, a "hands-off" policy had left the administration of prisons to criminal justice officials. Yet, as prisoners filed cases that slowly revealed the human rights abuses that were common throughout the criminal justice system, the tide began to turn. Cases like *Holt v. Sarver* in Arkansas drew attention to issues of prison violence. The Arkansas court ruled that the entire prison system constituted cruel and unusual punishment after investigators discovered that inmates were routinely beaten, packed into unlivable living quarters, and forced to work excruciating shifts on the prison farms while being undernourished and constantly threatened with violence. This case, and others, led to a vast federal assessment of state prison systems. By the early 1980s, dozens of prisons were under federal court supervision for violating the rights of inmates. Despite all this, prisons already had started to operate as industries and the abolitionist expressions of anti-incarceration advocates were lost amid the "law and order" rhetoric that eventually helped elect Ronald Reagan in 1980.

Groups like CAPS and PREAP suffered because they did not understand the processes of globalization and deindustrialization taking place concurrently with prison expansion. Just as the aftermath of 19th-century emancipation reproduced the racial hierarchies of slavery in the structures of the criminal justice system, during the post–World War II period new economic and social configurations provided fresh impetus to the acceleration of prison building. Ruth Wilson Gilmore traces how these transformations—globalization, reindustrialization, imperialism, and racism—converged in the 1960s and 1970s. Unfortunately, activists inside and outside prisons refused to see these changes as "forces," but instead as choices that emerged from state reconciliation with capital. Prisons were the physical structures called upon to help respond to the chaos unleashed by the globalization of capital and they were supposed to (at least in theory) contain the array of struggles waged against these processes by people of color, immigrants, and the poor. . . .

Previous prison abolition movements seem to have understood mass incarceration as a class-based injustice perpetrated against the working classes and the poor. Yet as Angela Davis has pointed out, prison abolitionists have much to gain from building coalitions with those who focus on the abolition of "whiteness" as a way to approach the effects of racism embodied in the prison-industrial complex. Because racism has played such a central role in the proliferation of prisons and the irrational fear of crime (helping to assure passage of legislation like California's Proposition 21), imagining abolitionism requires us to envision the elimination of the privileges of whiteness, as well as a divestment of public resources from prison building. Because the uneven distribution of state resources that has contributed to the prison-industrial complex has been driven by racism, movements that challenge the terms of mass imprisonment will necessarily be joined with antiracist movements, which acknowledge the continued racialization of state resource distribution.

The echoes of slavery still reverberate throughout the prison state; earlier this year [2000], the Wackenhut corporation announced a new contract to build a federal prison on the site of a former slave plantation in North Carolina. This brings us back to the question of the feasibility of anti-incarceration movements. In the age of Proposition 21, the Super-Max, the rapid reinvigoration of the death penalty, globalization, and the convergence of the two political parties in the U.S. around punishment as a corrective to unemployment and race problems, can prison abolitionism be heard? The answer is "yes," for the very starkness of this moment breathes new life into abolitionism as a counter to reforms that accept the terms of human destruction and devastation inherent in contemporary prisons. Throughout the U.S., and increasingly throughout the world, prison abolitionism is finding new life as local movements against prison construction, mandatory minimum sentences, and the criminalization of youth are created out of the very communities they decimate. This year, as Western European nations and corporations finally have been forced to accept their complicity in the use of slave labor under Nazism, perhaps the issue of reparations for slavery in the U.S. will at last gain legitimacy in a country that has institutionalized new forms of slavery rather than vanquish bondage completely.

Slavery in U.S. Suburbs

Paul Vitello

*Though many people assume that slavery ended with the ratifi-
cation of the Thirteenth Amendment, involuntary servitude is
present in twenty-first-century America. The New York Times
writer Paul Vitello chronicles the harrowing story of two women
forced to work in the home of an affluent Long Island, New
York, couple for five years. He details how the women endured
countless horrors at the hands of the two perfume manufacturers
during their time in the home. Witnesses claim that the women
were beaten and half-starved, he says. Vitello argues that though
many people might believe this case is isolated, more and more
incidents of involuntary servitude are being brought out of the
shadows and into the light. Experts cited by Vitello explain that
modern-day slavery is not only more common than most Americans realize but also a crime that often goes unpunished because
of a lack of evidence.*

T he two tiny Indonesian women know just a handful of
English words. They know Windex. Fantastik (the cleanser,
not the adjective). They know the words Master and Missus,
which they were taught to use in addressing the Long Island
couple they served as live-in help for five years in the sylvan
North Shore hamlet of Muttontown, New York.

Their employers, Varsha Sabhnani, 45, and her husband,
Mahender, 51, naturalized citizens from India, have been on
trial in U.S. District Court here for the past month. They are
charged with what the federal criminal statutes refer to as involuntary servitude and peonage, or, in the common national
parlance since 1865, the crime of keeping slaves.

The two women, the government charged in its indictment, were victims of "modern-day slavery."

Paul Vitello, "From Stand in Long Island Slavery Case, a Snapshot of a Hidden U.S.
Problem," *The New York Times*, December 3, 2007. Reprinted with permission.

A Crime That Often Goes Unpunished

It is a rarely prosecuted crime. But since passage of the 2000 federal Trafficking Victims Protection Act, prosecutions have increased from less than a handful nationwide per year to about a dozen. The law is probably best known for its focus on prostitution and child-sex traffickers; yet in the last few years, in a few highly publicized cases like the Sabhnanis', federal and state task forces set up to deal with sex trafficking have also begun to focus on the exploitation of domestic workers.

In 2006, the wife of a Saudi prince was convicted in Boston for keeping two house servants for three years in virtual slavery. In 2005, two doctors in Wisconsin were convicted of holding a Philippine woman as an indentured servant for 20 years. Federal prosecutors won convictions in 2003 against a Maryland couple who kept a Brazilian woman in their home as a servant for 15 years, paying her nothing.

In the Long Island case, prosecutors say the two Indonesian women were made to sleep in closets of the sprawling, multimillion-dollar home of their employers. They were forced to work day and night, threatened, tortured, beaten with rolling pins and brooms, deprived of adequate food and never allowed out of the house except to take out the garbage.

The defense lawyers, who are scheduled to begin their case on Monday, have characterized the two women as liars, practitioners of witchcraft, and inventors of a false claim designed to win them fast-track advantages that federal immigration law grants certain victims of torture and abuse. Whatever injuries the women may have suffered, the lawyers said, were self-inflicted in the practice of a traditional Indonesian folk cure known as kerokan.

Advocacy groups, prosecutors and researchers who study labor trafficking say domestic workers are as vulnerable to exploitation as sex workers, and in some ways even harder to reach.

"The domestic servant cases are often the most brutal because of the total isolation in which these women are kept for years and years," said Cathleen Caron, executive director of Global Workers Justice Alliance, a New York–based advocacy group that provides legal help to exploited migrant workers. She has been watching the Sabhnani case with interest, she said.

The Indonesian women in the Long Island case are identified by the government only by their first names, Samirah and Enung. They are 51 and 47 years old, respectively. Each stands less than five feet tall. In their many hours of translated testimony and cross-examination so far, halted occasionally by fits of sobbing, they have told a grim tale at odds with every notion of modern life in the United States.

The Sabhnanis, who are perfume manufacturers with relatives and business contacts in Indonesia, lured them from their jobs and families in Jakarta in 2002 with false promises, they say, and then subjected them to relentless abuse until Samirah ran away in May [2007].

Exposing a Hidden Population

Regardless of the jury's verdict, the case has raised the profile of a population, mostly of women, hidden in the folds of some very affluent American households, according to advocates for exploited workers.

Claudia Flores, a staff lawyer for the American Civil Liberties Union who recently represented three Indian women kept in involuntary servitude by foreign diplomats in Washington, said foreign workers unfamiliar with American culture and language, already vulnerable, are pushed beyond the pale by isolation.

"Many times, they are forbidden to talk to people who come into the house," Ms. Flores said. "If there are two of them, they are often forbidden to talk to each other. Their phone calls are monitored. They are not allowed to go anywhere unaccompanied. We are only seeing the women who are lucky enough and capable enough to find assistance. What we see is really only the tip of the iceberg."

A report released in July [2007] by the federal State Department, "Pursuing a Dream and Finding a Nightmare," said the exploitation of women as domestic workers in the United States and abroad was a crime that has "largely gone unpunished for too long."

The report, written by research staff in the department's Office to Monitor and Combat Trafficking in Persons, underlined the government's concern for "unskilled women from developing countries, particularly women working as domestics," who it said often "fall victim to conditions of servitude in developed destination countries, including the United States."

Jodi Bobb, a U.S. Justice Department spokeswoman, said the Long Island slavery case was one of about 100 prosecutions for involuntary servitude or labor trafficking since passage of the 2000 anti-trafficking law. Not all of them involved domestic workers, she said, but that number represents a twofold increase in such prosecutions compared with the seven years before 2000.

The number of migrant domestic servants living in involuntary servitude in the United States is a matter for guessing, but there are some well-informed guesses. The State Department report estimated that the total number of people trafficked to the United States annually was 15,000 to 20,000.

The figures do not distinguish between people trafficked for prostitution or factory, farm or domestic work. But advocates including Ms. Flores and Ms. Caron, based on hundreds of cases that filter through their agencies, estimated that domestic workers accounted for about one-third of the total.

In other words, 5,000 to 7,000 migrant domestic servants take jobs each year in homes where they are highly vulnerable to abuse by their employers, they say.

Broken Promises

Whether or not they live in conditions as violent as Samirah and Enung claim to have suffered, almost all are uneducated women from the world's poorest countries, according to the State Department report. Some are children.

They may sign employment contracts promising wages that seem princely in their home countries—Samirah and Enung agreed to $100 a month, for instance—but which severely limit their options here. The temporary visas they obtain with their new employers' help usually expire after three to six months, giving employers ammunition to threaten the servants with certain arrest if they leave the house.

"Who would do this to another human being?" said Suzanne Tomatore, director of the Immigrant Women and Children Project of the New York City Bar Association, which has assisted dozens of migrant domestic servants. "All kinds of people. Doctors, lawyers, professionals, business people, diplomats—the only thing the employers have in common as a group is they all have the resources to pay someone a fair wage, but they choose not to."

Ms. Tomatore said prosecutions were difficult for obvious reasons: language and cultural barriers. Fear. In many cases, depression. One of her clients, a 24-year-old woman, had been a domestic servant in one household since she was 6. "She had never been to school," said Ms. Tomatore, who would not identify the woman or the employers except to say they were diplomats from an African nation who have since left. The woman was given permanent legal immigration status. She works in an office.

During the Long Island trial, sobbing sometimes overtook Samirah as she described the tortures she was subjected to— being forced to run up and down stairs until exhausted, to eat whole hot chili peppers, to stand still while "the Missus" scalded her with boiling hot water. Sometimes the sobbing overtook Enung, who described being forced to help perform some of those tortures on Samirah.

The case is unusual, advocates say, because there were other witnesses to corroborate some of the women's claims. Among them was a woman who worked for Mr. Sabhnani's perfume company, which is based in an office attached to the Muttontown house. She said she was shocked one day to see Samirah crawling up the basement stairs, bleeding from the forehead. The woman testified that Samirah and Enung told her that Mrs. Sabhnani had beaten her.

A landscape contractor testified that Enung approached him furtively one morning, raggedly dressed, pointing to her stomach and uttering one of her few English words: "Doughnut," he recalled her saying. "Doughnut." He gave her the half-dozen doughnuts he had in his truck.

"Thank you, thank you, thank you," she cried as she ran back toward the big house, he said.

Appendices

Appendix A

The Amendments to the U.S. Constitution

Amendment I: Freedom of Religion, Speech, Press, Petition, and
                  Assembly (ratified 1791)

Amendment II: Right to Bear Arms (ratified 1791)

Amendment III: Quartering of Soldiers (ratified 1791)

Amendment IV: Freedom from Unfair Search and Seizures
                  (ratified 1791)

Amendment V: Right to Due Process (ratified 1791)

Amendment VI: Rights of the Accused (ratified 1791)

Amendment VII: Right to Trial by Jury (ratified 1791)

Amendment VIII: Freedom from Cruel and Unusual Punishment
                  (ratified 1791)

Amendment IX: Construction of the Constitution (ratified 1791)

Amendment X: Powers of the States and People (ratified 1791)

Amendment XI: Judicial Limits (ratified 1795)

Amendment XII: Presidential Election Process (ratified 1804)

Amendment XIII: Abolishing Slavery (ratified 1865)

Amendment XIV: Equal Protection, Due Process, Citizenship for All
                  (ratified 1868)

The Amendments to the U.S. Constitution

Amendment XV: Race and the Right to Vote (ratified 1870)
Amendment XVI: Allowing Federal Income Tax (ratified 1913)
Amendment XVII: Establishing Election to the U.S. Senate
                     (ratified 1913)
Amendment XVIII: Prohibition (ratified 1919)
Amendment XIX: Granting Women the Right to Vote (ratified 1920)
Amendment XX: Establishing Term Commencement for Congress
                     and the President (ratified 1933)
Amendment XXI: Repeal of Prohibition (ratified 1933)
Amendment XXII: Establishing Term Limits for U.S. President
                     (ratified 1951)
Amendment XXIII: Allowing Washington, D.C., Representation in the
                     Electoral College (ratified 1961)
Amendment XXIV: Prohibition of the Poll Tax (ratified 1964)
Amendment XXV: Presidential Disability and Succession
                     (ratified 1967)
Amendment XXVI: Lowering the Voting Age (ratified 1971)
Amendment XXVII: Limiting Congressional Pay Increases
                     (ratified 1992)

Appendix B

Court Cases Relevant to the Thirteenth Amendment

Dred Scott v. Sandford, 1856

In this case, decided before the adoption of the Thirteenth Amendment, Dred Scott, a slave who traveled to a free territory with his master and lived a free life after the death of his master, sued for his freedom. The Court ruled that African Americans were not considered "citizens" under the Constitution, and they therefore had no right to sue in a court of law.

Blyew v. U.S., 1871

This case was the first case brought to the Supreme Court involving the Civil Rights Act ruling of 1866. This case was brought to the Court after white men murdered African American men, and the two witnesses to the crime—African American men—were forbidden to testify against white people according to Kentucky law.

Civil Rights Cases, 1883

The Court ruled that the Civil Rights Act of 1875 and the equal protection clauses of the Fifth and Fourteenth Amendments apply only to state and federal actions. The Court held that private acts of racial discrimination are private matters that cannot be corrected through legislation.

Plessy v. Ferguson, 1896

With its decision in *Plessy*, the Court ruled that "separate but equal" facilities were constitutional and did not violate the Thirteenth and Fourteenth Amendments. This decision enabled states to pass laws legalizing segregation.

Slaughter-House Cases, 1872

This case sprung from three cases involving three slaughter-houses that were suing because of a piece of Louisiana legislation allowing slaughterhouses to be regulated by the states. The butchers claimed that they were involved in involuntary servitude because they had to work for the state, but the Supreme Court ruled that the Thirteenth and Fourteenth Amendments protected only former slaves, severely limiting the scope of these amendments.

Butcher's Union Co. v. Crescent City Co., 1884
In this Slaughter-House Case, the Court overturned its previous decision, holding that the slaughterhouse monopoly in Louisiana violated the Thirteenth and Fourteenth Amendments.

Robertson v. Baldwin, 1897
This case justified forced duty imposed on sailors, stating that sailors surrendered their personal liberty during their contracts. In the dissenting opinion, Justice Harlan states that the Thirteenth Amendment allows involuntary servitude only for punishment, and that slavery should exist in no form in the United States.

Clyatt v. U.S., 1905
In this peonage case, the Supreme Court ruled that servitude could be imposed punishment for payment of a debt because peonage implies involuntary servitude. This ruling states that if a person is imposed servitude as payment of a debt, he or she can end the servitude voluntarily by paying the debt.

Bailey v. Alabama, 1911
In this peonage case, Alonzo Bailey, an impoverished African American man, was forced to work after he agreed to work for twelve dollars per month, received an advance, and did not work or refund the money. The Court held that forcing a person to work for taking money for work not performed is the same as indentured servitude because it requires a person to work instead of finding the person guilty of a crime.

U.S. v. Reynolds, 235 U.S. 133, 1914
This case was another peonage case of Alabama, which struck down Alabama laws requiring work to repay a debt or obligation.

Butler v. Perry, 1916
The U.S. Supreme Court ruled that a Florida ordinance requiring every "able-bodied male person" to work on roads and bridges was not unconstitutional under the Thirteenth and Fourteenth Amendments because men could choose to pay a reasonable fine not more than fifty dollars rather than doing the work.

Arver v. U.S., 1918
The Court ruled that forcing military service is not unconstitutional under the Thirteenth and Fourteenth Amendments because Articles 1 and 8 of the Constitution allow Congress the power to raise and support armies, but not for longer than a term of two years.

Taylor v. Ga., 1942
In this peonage case, the Court held Georgia laws requiring work to repay a debt or obligation unconstitutional.

Pollock v. Williams, 1944
The Court ruled that a Florida statute, which held a person guilty of a misdemeanor for receiving an advance in exchange for agreeing to render services and then failing to render the services, is unconstitutional.

Hurd v. Hodge, 1948
In this case, legislation that denied the sale of certain real estate to African Americans was held unconstitutional.

Brown v. The Board of Education of Topeka, Kansas, 1954
The Court's decision in *Brown* repealed the *Plessy* decision, stating that separate facilities were inherently unequal, therefore violating the Thirteenth and Fourteenth Amendments. This decision illegalized segregation.

Atlanta Motel v. U.S., 1964
In this case, a Georgia motel sued, contending that provisions of the Civil Rights Act of 1964 that forced motels to rent to African Americans amounted to involuntary servitude. The Court upheld the Civil Rights Act of 1964, stating that the act does not impose involuntary servitude.

Jones v. Alfred H. Mayer Co., 1968
This case ruled that an act of Congress was constitutional and allowed Congress to regulate the private sale of property. This decision barred, and sought to prevent, racial discrimination in the sale of private property.

Swann v. Charlotte-Mecklenburg Board of Education, 1971
The Supreme Court ruled that mandatory busing, involving busing students outside of their usual school districts, was an appropriate remedy to desegregate schools in a timely manner. With this case, the Court inadvertently created problems with inner-city schools due to white Americans moving to the suburbs to avoid desegregation.

McDonald v. Santa Fe Trail Transportation Co., 1976
In this case, white employees of the Santa Fe Trail Transportation Co. sued after they were discharged for certain behavior, but an African American employee was not discharged. In its decision, the Court ruled that the Civil Rights Act of 1866 applies to all persons.

Memphis v. Greene, 1981
This case involved a decision of Memphis, Tennessee, to close a road that connected a predominantly white neighborhood and a predominantly black neighborhood. In the majority decision, the Court held that the road closing did not qualify as a "badge of slavery."

Toibb v. Radloff, 1991
In this bankruptcy case, the Supreme Court ruled that if a worker's wages are garnished to benefit creditors, the worker is compelled to work for the creditor. This therefore qualifies as involuntary servitude, violating the Thirteenth Amendment.

For Further Research

Alice D. Adams, *The Neglected Period of Anti-Slavery in America, 1808–1831*. Williamstown, MA: Corner House Publishers, 1973. First published 1908 by Radcliffe College.

Ira Berlin, *Many Thousands Gone: The First Two Centuries of Slavery in North America*. Cambridge, MA: Belknap Press of Harvard University Press, 1998.

Ira Berlin, Barbara J. Fields, Steven F. Miller, Joseph P. Reidy, and Leslie S. Rowland, eds., *Free at Last: A Documentary History of Slavery, Freedom, and the Civil War*. New York: New Press, 1992.

Don E. Fehrenbacher, *Slavery, Law, and Politics: The Dred Scott Case in Historical Perspective*. New York: Oxford University Press, 1981.

John H. Franklin, *Race and History: Selected Essays, 1938–1988*. Baton Rouge: Louisiana State University Press, 1989.

Kenneth S. Greenberg, ed., *The Confessions of Nat Turner and Related Documents*. Boston: Bedford Books of St. Martin's Press, 1996.

William Harper, James H. Hammond, William G. Simms, and Thomas R. Dew, *The Pro-Slavery Argument, as Maintained by the Most Distinguished Writers of the Southern States*. Philadelphia: Lippincott, Grambo, & Co., 1853.

Peter Kolchin, *American Slavery, 1619–1877*. Ed. Eric Foner. New York: Hill and Wang, 1993.

Ann J. Lane, ed., *The Debate over Slavery: Stanley Elkins and His Critics*. Urbana: University of Illinois Press, 1971.

Horace Mann, *Slavery: Letters and Speeches; The Anti-Slavery Crusade in America*. New York: Arno Press, 1969. First published 1851 by B.B. Mussey & Co.

Kenneth M. Stampp and Leon F. Litwack, eds., *Reconstruction: An Anthology of Revisionist Writings*. Baton Rouge: Louisiana State University Press, 1969.

John L. Thomas, ed., *Slavery Attacked: The Abolitionist Crusade*. Englewood Cliffs, NJ: Prentice-Hall, 1965.

William L. Van Deburg, *Slavery & Race in American Popular Culture*. Madison: University of Wisconsin Press, 1984.

Joel Williamson, *After Slavery: The Negro in South Carolina During Reconstruction, 1861–1877*. New York: Norton, 1975.

Theodore B. Wilson, *The Black Codes of the South*. Tuscaloosa: University of Alabama Press, 1965.

Raymond A. Winbush, *Should America Pay?: Slavery and the Raging Debate on Reparations*. New York: Amistad, 2003.

Howard Zinn, *A People's History of the United States, 1492–Present*. Rev. ed. New York: HarperPerennial, 1995.

Periodicals

Ira Berlin, "American Slavery in History and Memory and the Search for Social Justice," *Journal of American History*, vol. 90, no. 4, March 2004.

Christopher Bryant, "Stopping Time: The Pro-Slavery and 'Irrevocable' Thirteenth Amendment," *Harvard Journal of Law & Public Policy*, vol. 26, no. 2, Spring 2003.

William M. Carter Jr., "A Thirteenth Amendment Framework for Combating Racial Profiling," *Harvard Civil Rights-Civil Liberties Law Review*, vol. 39, no. 1, Winter 2004.

David Brion Davis, "The Central Fact of American History," *American Heritage*, vol. 56, no. 1, February/March 2005.

Allen C. Guelzo, "How Abe Lincoln Lost the Black Vote: Lincoln and Emancipation in the African American Mind," *Journal of the Abraham Lincoln Association*, vol. 25, no. 1, Winter 2004. www.historycooperative.org.

Robert Harrison, "An Experimental Station for Lawmaking: Congress and the District of Columbia, 1862–1878," *Civil War History*, vol. 53, no. 1, March 2007.

David Livingstone, "The Emancipation Proclamation, the Declaration of Independence, and the Presidency: Lincoln's Model of Statesmanship," *Perspectives on Political Science*, vol. 28, no. 4, Fall 1999.

Alton H. Maddox Jr., "Revisiting Dred Scott on March 7 in NYC," *New York Amsterdam News*, vol. 98, no. 10, March 1, 2007.

New York Times, "Mississippi: The Attitude of the State and the Explanation; The Civil Rights Bill Declared Unconstitutional by a State Court," October 26, 1866. http://query.nytimes.com.

———, "No 'Badges of Slavery,'" June 22, 1968.

———, "Supreme Court Roundup: Rights Plea by Memphis to Be Heard; Atlanta Schools Alimony Rights Information Act Lawyers' Conflicts," May 13, 1980. http://select.nytimes.com.

Jeremy Redmon and Lindsay Kastner, "Lincoln Statue Unveiled," *Times-Dispatch*, April 6, 2003.

Web Sites

Digital History: America's Reconstruction: People and Politics After the Civil War, www.digitalhistory.uh.edu. The Web site provides a timeline leading up to and following America's Civil War, with links that include details about people who affected America's Reconstruction.

Freedmen and Southern Society Project: Documents from Freedom: A Documentary History of Emancipation, 1861–1867, www.history.umd.edu. The Web site provides links to transcriptions and images of important documents from the Civil War.

Lincoln Institute Presents Mr. Lincoln and Freedom, www
.mrlincolnandfreedom.org. The Web site provides a timeline and history leading up to the Thirteenth Amendment, including before, during, and after the Civil War.

Slavery and the Making of America, www.pbs.org. The Web
site provides a timeline—spanning more than 250
years—of historical events concerning slavery in America's
history.

Index